CHILDREN DON'T START WARS

DAVID GRIBBLE

Published by Peace News
5 Caledonian Road, London N1 9DY
www.peacenews.info

© David Gribble, 2010
ISBN: 978-0-946409-14-3
Cover by Emily Johns
Layout by Martin Parker at www.silbercow.co.uk

Printed by Catford Print Centre
1-3 Bellingham Road, London SE6 2PN
www.catfordprint.co.uk

Wally (aged five):	People don't feel the same as grown-ups.
Teacher:	Do you mean "children don't"?
Wally:	Because grown-ups don't remember when they were little. They're already an old person.

From *Wally's Stories*, by Vivian Gussin Paley

With much ado I was corrupted, and made to learn the dirty devices of this world, which I now unlearn, and become, as it were, a little child again that I may enter into the Kingdom of God.

From *Centuries of Meditations*, by Thomas Traherne

I would like to express my gratitude to the following people, for information, translation, inspiration, criticism, encouragement, help with sources and/or correcting my versions of their ideas:

Alison Stallibrass, Primrose Somme, Jenifer Smith, Mimsy Sadofsky, Sarah McCrum, Dick Kitto, Mary John, Jill Hannam, Hanrahan Higgs, Jonathan Franklin, Joe Finbow, Kristin Eskeland, Judy Dunn, Simon Davies and of course my own family, in particular Lynette, Emma and Nathan.
— *David Gribble*

Except for one from *L'Art d'Être Grandpère* by Victor Hugo, The epigraphs throughout are from William Wordsworth's *Ode: Intimations of Immortality from Recollections of Early Childhood* (1804).

CONTENTS

CHAPTER ONE

THE GLORY AND THE FRESHNESS OF A DREAM

There was a time when meadow, grove and stream,
    The earth, and every common sight
To me did seem
    Apparelled in celestial light,
The glory and the freshness of a dream.
It is not now as it hath been of yore-
    Turn wheresoe'er I may,
    By night or day,
The things which I have seen I now can see no more.

William Wordsworth

As we get older we not only hear and see less well and become physically and mentally less agile but we also become less good at making rational moral decisions. Our capacity for empathy begins to decline at the latest in early childhood, the suppression of altruism is taught at school and selfish conformity grows as we adapt to adult society.

It is obvious that our physical skills decline with age and, although it is an unpopular idea, there is incontrovertible evidence that our intellects also begin to become less alert, flexible and reliable after the age of about twenty-five. Although there is no reason to suppose that our moral sensitivity should be exempt from this general decline, the notion that children might be morally superior to their elders arouses an indignation that is sometimes close to fury.

A nineteen-year-old former member of the Chicago gang culture gave me an illustration of the corrupting effect of age and power when I visited the Doctor Albizu Campos Puerto Rican High School, where many of the students were former gang members.

"The old ones," he said, "is what you call the OGs, they call them Original Gangsters. In a gang once you pass the limit of twenty-one you become one of the big-heads, you become, like, wiser, you're no more use to them because you're already old. To them you're old, you know, you can't be a soldier no more. Mainly the soldiers are all young people, I mean eleven, twelve, thirteen, real young kids that are all out there killing each other over a street that doesn't even belong to them. They're fighting over things that they don't even know what they're really fighting for. They don't know the meaning of the fight that they do, you know, the struggles that are happening to them. It's bad, because I see all these shorties dying over things that they don't even know about... And mainly what I don't understand is that all that violence is going on while the heads of every single gang is always smoking with each other, with all the heads, they're always having sessions and making business with each other, while youngsters are out there killing each other and everything."

The children are used by the OGs in the same way as governments use young men. In national wars of aggression it is the twenty-year-olds who are sent out to kill one another while the politicians stay safely at home, supported by businessmen who do deals. This extreme example of older people leading younger ones into the ultimate immorality which is war can only be explained by an acquired blindness or indifference to the suffering of others. Children don't start wars. Adults do.

The conventional view is that adults have a monopoly on wisdom, and children's opinions are not to be taken seriously. Those of us who disagree are ashamed to express an opposite view for fear of seeming naive, and most of us do not even put this view into words in our own minds. Nevertheless it is close to the surface of the consciousness of our present age; once you take it seriously you find confirmation in unexpected quarters.

I first framed this opposite view in words after I heard a short speech made by a twelve-year-old Rwandan girl at the Rio environmental conference in 1992. It seemed like a new discovery, but to my surprise I found on reflection that I had probably known it all my life. I certainly knew about it at the age of twenty, when I wrote down an approximation in a diary. In spite of this, and in spite of the fact that my whole life had been subconsciously directed by this very idea, I had never before dared to express it. Like so many other people, I had suppressed it because it seemed outrageous.

Hearing the Rwandan girl's speech was the culmination of a variety of reading and experience. The first seven chapters of my book describe this background. Then, after quoting the speech and stating my theme briefly once again, I answer the more obvious objections, analyse some of the differences between children's and adults' moral stances, offer further support from psychological research, describe places where children have flourished without moral standards being imposed by adults and in the final chapter draw attention to the implications.

I shall start cautiously by introducing myself and discussing early childhood memories – a few of my own but mostly other people's.

A Personal Introduction

In 1992 I retired from teaching. Because of the sort of person I am, and because of the sort of school I taught in, I have had a closer relationship with children than most teachers do. I retired at sixty, earlier than was strictly necessary, because the kind of relationship I needed in order to teach as I thought right had become impossible.

For the last five years I had been teaching at Sands School, in south Devon. It is an independent day school where children and staff share responsibility for all decisions, share the domestic chores and maintenance jobs and share the whole social space – there is no staff room. Sands is not a Utopia, but it is always trying to become one. It was a school that suited me perfectly, but I became too old.

Towards the end, if I joined in with children's games on the terrace I could only be a lumbering outsider who had to be treated with consideration. My opinions about films or television programmes were the irrelevant opinions of an old man. I didn't like the music the children liked, I dressed in comical clothes and I could disperse a group of chatting children in a few minutes simply by sitting down to join the chat. This is not to say that I was not fond of the children, nor that they were not fond of me; it is not even to say that we did not understand one another; it was just that it was finally plain that our interests and customs were not the same, that we belonged to different cultures.

I had had a similar insight twenty-five years earlier, when my own children were going to nursery school. When they played imaginative games, pushing cars along or talking to toys, I was unable to join in because I did not understand the principles of the games; all I could do was interfere and play on my own terms. Ten-year-olds, on the other hand, were able to join in effectively, and both they and the younger children enjoyed themselves.

Other People's Memories

Physical decline with age is observable and inevitable. You have to retire from the world of international sport twenty or thirty years earlier than you have to retire from teaching. In some respects this decline starts very much earlier than we like to think. Over a lifespan many organs, such as the heart, kidneys, brain and lungs show a gradual decline. The numbers of olfactory and optic nerve fibres decrease. The rate of wound healing decreases with age, rapidly at first and then more slowly in older people. Post-mortems on Vietnam soldiers revealed that arteries begin to fur up early. Accommodation of the lens of the eye decreases at a constant rate from the age of five.

However obvious any particular aspect of this decline may be, most people make an effort to avoid seeing it. An example of this is the way the

Encyclopaedia Britannica tells us that hearing does not change much with age "for the tones of frequencies usually encountered in daily life" (though it admits that above the age of fifty we begin to lose the ability to perceive the higher frequencies). Of course most of us can hear the tones of frequencies we encounter in daily life; if we didn't we wouldn't encounter them. Frequencies higher than those encountered in daily life by the middle-aged begin to disappear from our range while we are still children.

I observed this being demonstrated by a science teacher at Sands School. A group of people of various ages listened while she played a recording of a sound too high-pitched for the human ear, which gradually descended until we could hear it. We were told to raise our hands as soon as we could hear it. I watched while the youngest children raised their hands, and heard nothing. The older children raised their hands. I heard nothing. The staff began to raise their hands, strictly in order of age. I heard nothing. And then, suddenly, after all that silence, I heard the noise, loud and clear. This experiment is presumably conducted in many schools, but surprisingly little is made of it.

For some reason it is quite happily accepted that children can hear bats squeak and the middle-aged can't, but the idea that there is a whole range of sounds that we cannot hear, sensations that we can no longer experience and colours that we can no longer distinguish we find almost incredible. If something can be neither seen nor heard nor felt then it does not have any concrete existence. Those of us who are beginning to need glasses will know the astonishment of finding something by touch which we knew was not there because we had already looked. Nevertheless, it is true that our senses begin to deteriorate in some respects long before we are adults, and the pace of deterioration gradually accelerates. Children really do see and hear things in a way that is no longer possible for adults. When Wordsworth wrote "The things which I have seen I now can see no more" he was telling the literal truth.

They don't just see and hear them differently, they appreciate them differently. This is Gwen Raverat, Charles Darwin's grand-daughter, writing about her early childhood in her book *Period Piece*:

> For instance, the path in front of the veranda was made of large round water-worn pebbles, from some sea beach. They were not loose, but

stuck down tight in moss and sand, and were black and shiny, as if they had been polished. I adored those pebbles. I mean literally, *adored,* worshipped. This passion made me feel quite sick sometimes. And it was adoration that I felt for the foxgloves at Down, and for the stiff red clay out of the Sandwalk clay-pit; and for the beautiful white paint on the nursery floor. This kind of feeling hits you in the stomach, and in the ends of your fingers, and it is probably the most important thing in life. Long after I have forgotten all my human loves, I shall still remember the smell of a gooseberry leaf, or the feel of the wet grass on my bare feet; or the pebbles in the path. In the long run it is this feeling that makes life worth living, this which is the driving force behind the artist's need to create.

Of course, there were things to worship everywhere. I can remember feeling quite desperate with love for the blisters in the dark red paint on the nursery window-sills at Cambridge, but at Down there were more things to worship than anywhere else in the world.

I am going to quote often from autobiographies in these first two chapters, not because the quotations I shall use offer any proof – after all, the authors' experiences might be totally untypical or even wrongly remembered – nor because the authors are authorities on psychological development, because none of them are, nor because they command general respect, because not all of them do; I am going to quote autobiographies because the authors describe childhood experiences at first hand, because the experiences they describe are not unfamiliar to the rest of us, and because the accumulation of examples in itself is not without weight. Of course I never saw Gwen Raverat's adored pebbles, or the blisters in the red paint that she loved so desperately, but there were things that I loved in the same way. The sensation that occurs to me at the moment is of the smell of woodsmoke in my grandmother's drawing-room. I accept the strength of Gwen Raverat's emotion, but not because it can be proved. After all, there is no way of proving that a given thought has passed through anyone's mind; all that can be said is that it seems likely to have done so, it seems to fit in with the pattern of one's own personal memories.

Gwen Raverat actually says that the kind of feeling she experienced "is probably the most important thing in life." Adults, too, occasionally have a sense of overwhelming and entirely spontaneous love for an object, but it seems to get rarer with age.

Brenda Crowe, the first National Adviser to the Pre-School Playgroups Association, used to ask parents who came to her seminars for memories of their early childhood. Some of these memories appear in her book, *Play is a Feeling*. These are not necessarily the memories of literate people who would later be able to write autobiographies, but they show the same intensity of feeling as that described by Gwen Raverat.

This first extract is from an account of a conversation with a woman whose background could hardly have been more different. She had been seriously mistreated as a child, both physically and emotionally.

It was a bitterly cold day and I was shut out of the house as usual in a cotton frock and knickers and without shoes. But I didn't feel the cold, I was playing in a deep cart-rut puddle and I was totally absorbed in what I was doing. I could feel the soft mud squelching up between my toes and round my ankles, and there was a worm floating in the puddle. I had a stick and I could make it wiggle as I stirred the water, then I stirred it up too hard and lost it, and then I stopped and the mud settled and it came back again. I forgot everything except that. It was *wonderful*. I just sat and drifted and didn't want to come back.

Another parent present at a seminar remembered walking hand in hand with her grandfather as he went to open his greenhouse, and a third remembered Sunday dinners with the whole family.

When we got there the windows were all grey and misty and I couldn't see in, which was funny, so I just stood still while Grandad unlocked the door. And then it happened, the door swung open and a rush of hot scented air was all around me, and the great big tomatoes shone red among the green leaves and I just stood there and it was the most wonderful moment of my whole life.

I can remember on Sundays the whole family came to dinner, all the grandparents and aunts and uncles and everyone. And afterwards everyone would go into the front room and my father used to take me on his lap, and they would talk. And I'd lie in his arms and drift off to sleep, and then the voices would come nearer and I'd wake up – then they'd fade away again. It was marvellous, just the warmth and the happiness, being held, and the voices coming and going and coming again in waves.

"Marvellous", "The most wonderful moment of my life", "It was *wonderful*. I just sat and drifted and didn't want to come back." Descriptions like these show a delight that we seem to lose as we get older. Oddly enough Brenda Crowe usually found it difficult at first to evoke any memories of early childhood, even when they were as pleasant as these; it was only with some prompting that people were able to revive what were plainly extremely valuable experiences. Perhaps the memory is suppressed. "Don't be silly," we may have been told. "It's only grandad's tomatoes. We'll be having them for tea soon." But surely we all have some such memories – lying flat on the turf and watching the clouds pass, stroking the scab on an old cut, seeing the sun shining pink and yellow right through our closed fingers, listening to footsteps on the stairs or watching the curtains over the window.

Eric Gill, in his *Autobiography*, writes of friendships as well as sensations.

> … Nevertheless, when I look back on the friendships of childhood they do not seem to differ in either quality or intensity from those of grown-up years. … And our enjoyments, though more limited in physical scope, were, within those limits, as intensely felt and consciously known as any that grown-up people can know – or, for I can only speak for myself, as intense and conscious as any that I have known since. We loved the flowers and the hills. We loved the sunsets and the birds and the beasts. We loved one another. And will anyone tell me that we did not love these things as much as we have learned to love them since?

It seems obvious to me that in those days we loved them more. Psychiatrists tell us that our early experiences are the most important in forming our characters. They do not usually say that this is in part because we feel them so much more deeply. A child's tears may sometimes be a social tool to achieve an end, but a child's grief, even if it is only over a lost toy, may well be profound, and a child's joy seems abundant enough for everyone who observes it to have a share. The fact that small children's joys and sorrows are often frequent and brief does not make them any less deeply felt. And of course not all children's sorrow is brief.

Eric Gill is bold enough to say "We loved one another." Autobiographers in general are much more likely to observe that they and their peers hated one another. In fact there was probably at least as much love as hatred, but it takes courage to confess to virtue. People often talk about original sin, but the idea that we also have an inborn understanding of right and wrong – original virtue, as A.S. Neill calls it – is seldom considered; the best we are likely to allow the infant is a wishy-washy innocence.

The standard view used to be that children were born evil and had to be educated to become good, but the moral direction of education is now sometimes questioned. "The chief thing that I learned at school," says Gwen Raverat in the book I have been quoting, "was how to tell lies."

Reasons for Choosing Autobiographies

I have chosen to quote autobiography rather than biography, not least because autobiographers attach much more importance to their own childhood. In Osbert Sitwell's four-volume autobiography he does not become an adult until volume three, and many writers, Gwen Raverat among them, have chosen to write books entirely about their own childhood. The sort of perception that I am picking out to use as illustration is not likely to be observable at second hand.

I have been seeking expressions of personal feelings and attitudes, rather than accounts of events. The authority of the event, though, the importance we attach to the apparent verifiability of accounts of things which are supposed to have happened, as opposed to accounts of things people may have felt, leads even autobiographers to tend to start with long historical and obviously researched descriptions of family background, and include plenty of amusing anecdotes of errors and minor humiliations that are more likely to be a part of family folklore than of personal memory. We are not confident of the accuracy of our recollections because so often we were not taken seriously at the time. Priscilla Napier was unusual in writing of the shame of being laughed at by adults for reasons she did not understand, but author after author commends this or that grandparent or adult friend of the family for listening seriously and talking to children as if they were the same age. Brenda Crowe also stresses how important it is for children that adults should take them seriously. All too often children learn not to expect to be taken seriously, and many adults seem to be cautious about relying too heavily on their own perceptions when they write about their childhoods, and to hedge themselves about with researched information and light self-mockery.

Another Kind of Recollection

Another person who spoke to Brenda Crowe told of a delight in setting things in order.

> An Irish journalist remembers kneeling under larch trees and raking the dry dust and fallen larch needles into runnels with wide-spaced fingers, then building up the ridges into parallel lines that were higher and deeper than before. Then came the gathering of larch cones and the careful grading of them by size, the smaller ones being set up on top of the front ridge, the medium ones on the second ridge, and the largest ones on the back ridge. 'I can remember the depth of concentration, and how terribly important it was that every cone was exactly the right size, and that they were placed exactly the same distance apart. It was immensely satisfying kneeling there in the sun, working so meticulously.'

That depth of concentration and immense satisfaction are things that we often seek as adults, and seldom find. Osbert Sitwell found an enlightenment that adults often work for years to achieve; it happened to him without effort when he was five.

> ... I ran to the edge of the precipice and stood there looking straight into the face of the evening sun. The light bathed the whole world in

its amber and golden rays, seeming to link up every object and every living thing, catching them in its warm, diaphanous net, so that I felt myself at one with my surroundings, part of this same boundless immensity of sea and sky and, even, of the detailed precision of the landscape, part of the general creation, divided from it by no barriers made by man or devil.

Sometimes I still faintly experience some such sensation when I stand on a shore and watch the sea, utterly insignificant before its vastness, and yet at the same time infinitely important because of being a part of the "boundless immensity", but when I was a child it was not a sensation but a certainty. I also particularly remember one occasion when I was recovering from an illness, lying in bed and knowing beyond question that the world was an utterly beautiful place and that whatever happened in the world it was in some incomprehensible way right. Awe at the beauty of tomatoes, or passionate delight in a worm floating in a puddle are the same kind of experience. You do not need the vastness of a seascape to give you a sense of the infinite.

Such experiences are often described as mystical or spiritual. I do not like such words. If you use them to describe your experiences, doctrinaire religion is likely to seize upon them as support for its elaborate creeds. The experiences relate either to something real, or to something imaginary. If they relate to something real then a description such as Osbert Sitwell's is complete and no further exegesis is needed.

Gwen Raverat said that the kind of experience she was describing, for instance her love for the bubbles in the paint, was probably the most important thing in life. This perhaps becomes more convincing when it is allied to Osbert Sitwell's rather more grandiose identification with his surroundings. He also felt united with "even the detailed precision of the landscape." Gwen Raverat's love and Osbert Sitwell's sense of unity may be different ways of describing the same experience.

I hope that the various quotations in this chapter have been enough to show that such experiences of total involvement are a perfectly normal part of childhood. What is extraordinary is that, although we may envy children their sharper senses, their liveliness and their capacity to be happy, we do not usually remember this sense of unity sufficiently clearly to regret its loss.

CHAPTER TWO

THE RISE AND FALL OF INTELLIGENCE

The memories quoted in the last chapter suggest that as we grow older we lose an affinity with the world around us. We also lose something in that area of intelligence that is measured by intelligence tests. This is a scientifically demonstrated deterioration that seems to be systematically ignored. There is very little about it in the psychology textbooks, and the psychologists who I have spoken to about it have tended either to claim ignorance, or to deny that the decline is either necessary or universal.

Because it is so little discussed, it is interesting to look at what David Wechsler, the psychologist who devised intelligence tests that are still commonly used today, seems to have proved as long ago as 1939. More recently Howard Gardner has propounded the theory that IQ measures only one of a number of different intelligences, and Daniel Goleman has shown that what he calls emotional intelligence is a better predictor of success in life than the intelligence measured by the Wechsler tests, but however you rate the importance of those tests, they certainly measure something. And it is not only Wechsler's conclusions that interest me, it is also the general reaction to them.

These are quotations from Wechsler himself:

Every human capacity after attaining a maximum begins an immediate decline. This decline is at first very slow but after a while increases perceptibly. The age at which the maximum is attained varies from ability to ability but seldom occurs beyond 30 and in most cases somewhere in the early 20's. Once the decline begins it progresses continually. ... Many of our intellectual abilities show a greater impairment with age than do our physical ones.

Hitherto the common view has been that our mental abilities, unlike our physical abilities, remain relatively unimpaired until rather late in life (senility), except as an occasional consequence of disease or traumatic injury. This was an unsubstantiated hypothesis tenable only so long as no facts were at hand to oppose it. But the view still persists even though such facts are now available. Most people, including scientists, hate to believe that they are not as mentally alert at 50 as they were at 20.

Few people are concerned when told that at 40 they cannot hear or fight as well as when they were 20, but are quite 'het up' when informed that they probably also cannot calculate or reason as well. There also exists a kind of hierarchy of relative values as regards the various mental abilities themselves. Professor Cattell long ago called attention to the fact that people are ever ready to complain about their bad memory, but seldom of their poor judgement or common sense.

Wechsler had tested groups of between 50 and 125 people in each of a number of age-ranges. He used a battery of tests to which he gave the names information, comprehension, arithmetic, digit span, similarities, picture arrangement, picture completion, block design, object assembly and digit symbol. Apart from arithmetic, these terms may need some explanation. Very roughly, the information test is a general knowledge quiz; the comprehension test asks for responses to fairly abstract questions such as "Why are laws necessary?"; digit span finds out how long a list of numbers you can remember after someone has read it out to you; similarities involves finding points in common between, say, a pear and an orange; picture arrangement is putting pictures in order so that they tell a story; picture completion requires you to notice what is missing from a picture, for instance the handle on a door; block design is using coloured blocks to copy a design on a card; object assembly is a kind of simple jigsaw or cut-up picture that you have to reassemble; and the digit symbol test is mainly a matter of speed, seeing how many numbers you can put into a given code within a given time.

The test on which the people in the oldest group (from 55 – 59 years old) did relatively worst was the picture arrangement, in which they did about as well as the nine-year-olds. They were also at the nine-year-old level on the digit symbol test. As might be expected, the test they did best on was the general knowledge test, in which they were as good as children of twelve.

On all the tests the highest scores came between the ages of fifteen and thirty, and most of the scores were pretty good by the age of thirteen. The chart below shows the ages at which the highest scores were achieved in the ten different tests.

	Number of tests in which the mean score for the group was:		
Age group	above 90%	above 95%	100% of the top score
13	6	1	0
14	8	2	0
15	9	4	2
16	9	6	1
17 – 19	9	5	4
20 – 24	10	9	4
25 – 29	10	6	1
30 – 34	6	0	0
35 – 39	4	0	0

The results of the different age-groups on two different tests, and on the test as a whole, are given in the diagram. The sub-tests chosen are the ones in which the oldest group did relatively best and relatively least well. In order to make comparison simpler, the mean scores for each group are given as percentages of the highest mean score attained by any group.

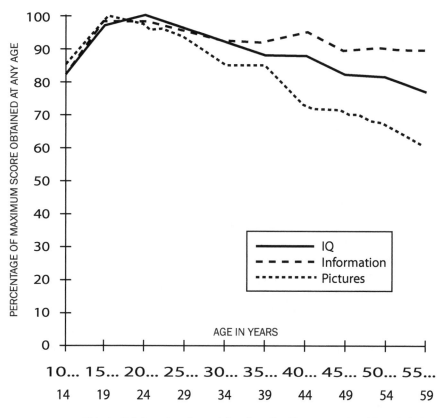

PERCENTAGE OF MAXIMUM SCORE OBTAINED AT ANY AGE

AGE IN YEARS

10... 15... 20... 25... 30... 35... 40... 45... 50... 55...
14   19   24   29   34   39   44   49   54   59

This graph is based on figures taken from *The Measurement and Appraisal of Adult Intelligence* by David Wechsler.

Scores have been re-calculated as percentages of the maximum score attained by any age group. This simplifies comparison of the results of different tests. (The numbers refer to ages).

In the different tests the 55 to 59-year-olds were at the following levels:

- twelve-year-old level – information, comprehension, picture completion
- eleven-year-old level – arithmetic, similarities, overall score
- ten-year-old level – digit span, block design, object assembly
- nine-year-old level – digit symbol, picture arrangement.

Reaction to the Findings

These figures are so startling that it is not surprising that most people refused to accept them. It was obvious that there were a lot of things fifty-year-olds could do that they had not been able to do when they were eleven, and ridiculous to argue that in that case there must have been even more things that they had been able to do when they were eleven but could no longer do now they were fifty.

Psychologists were eager to find fault with the tests and Wechsler's interpretation of them. It was suggested that intelligence declined only if it was not used, and that those who continued to use their brains retained their ability. Intelligence was divided up into various categories, so that it could be shown that older people retained at least some of their skills. The tests were criticised for being irrelevant and uninteresting to older people. It was discovered that each generation scored more highly than the previous one, so lower results for older people did not necessarily mean that their intelligence had declined, it just meant they had always been less intelligent.

This defence of the intelligence of the elderly had some effect, but it was not entirely successful. In 1977 Jack Botwinick summed up the position as follows:

> The 'no decline' side of the controversy ... catches the imagination and seems to please. Nevertheless, after reviewing the available literature, both recent and old, the conclusion here is that decline in intellectual ability is clearly part of the aging picture. ... [However] these declines may start later in life than heretofore thought, and they may be smaller in magnitude. They may also include fewer functions.

One theory that supports this statement is that intelligence can be divided into two broad types – crystallised intelligence and fluid intelligence. The former includes knowledge, skills, vocabulary and comprehension, and the later includes ability to solve new and unusual problems, reasoning, memory span and mental agility. Crystallised intelligence, to the relief of everyone over thirty, is believed to increase up until the age of about 80. Fluid intelligence, on the other hand, drops after the age of about 15.

The natural reaction of the middle-aged and elderly is to play down the importance of fluid intelligence. It is only when its benefits are absolutely obvious, as in computer programming or the currency markets, that young people are allowed to take their places at the top. If society were conducted rationally it would seem important that in most situations young and old should make decisions together. Unfortunately power goes with age, and old people are extremely reluctant to give it up. The days when Pitt the Younger could become Prime Minister at the age of twenty-four are past.

The relationship between age and power, however, is not relevant to my present argument. All I have sought to provide is a clear example of our irrational determination to deny all but the most self-evident superiorities of youth. Some aspects of intelligence certainly decline with age; nevertheless all evidence of decline with age is eagerly contested, not on scientific grounds but merely because, as Jack Botwinick says, "the 'no-decline' side of the controversy catches the imagination and seems to please."

How Babies Think

More recent research has produced new evidence of the superiority of the young brain. This is expressed in delightfully accessible terms by three American professors of psychology, Alison Gopnik from the University of California, Berkeley, Andrew Meltzoff from the University of Washington and Patricia Kuhl from the University of Washington, in their book *How Babies Think* (published in the USA as *The Scientist in the Crib*). "We are born with the ability to discover the secrets of the universe and of our own minds, and with the drive to explore and experiment until we do," they say, and later:

> Twenty-five years ago, when we were in college, we still heard respected psychologists proclaim that newborn babies had no cortex, that they had only the simplest automatic responses, that they were, in fact, slightly animate vegetables — carrots that could cry. Piaget himself thought that newborn babies had only reflexes...
> At first every new discovery about young babies, no matter how methodologically rigorous, was greeted by a kind of profound disbelief

that seemed to go beyond the usual scientific reluctance to accept new discoveries. It was as if the very idea that babies could think and believe, learn and know, was deeply unacceptable.

... the scientific battle was hard-fought. But by now it largely has been won. The sociological zeitgeist may have contributed to the victory, but the real weapons were the familiar scientific ones: careful and ingenious experiments, replications across laboratories, good arguments, and the conversion of the next generation.

Later in the book the authors give some more technical detail:

The brain's energy consumption reaches full adult levels at around two years of age. By three the little child's brain is actually twice as active as an adult brain. This bristling activity remains at twice the level of an adult until the child reaches the age of nine or ten. It begins to decline around then, but reaches adult levels only at about eighteen.

... At birth, each neuron in the cerebral cortex has around 2,500 synapses. The number of synapses reaches its peak at two to three years of age, when there about 15,000 synapses per neuron. This is actually many more than in an adult brain. Preschool children have brains that are literally more active, more connected, and much more flexible than ours.

...

All of this research is consistent with the idea that childhood is the time when we learn most and when our brains as well as our minds are most open to new experience. We saw that this is also the picture that comes out of psychological studies of development. Babies and young children are perpetually exploring and experimenting, testing out new theories and changing old theories when they learn something new. Although the process doesn't stop in adulthood, it certainly slows down.[1]

---

[1]   The last part of this sentence would be clearer if it read "does not fall to adult levels until about eighteen."

And all this leads to the conclusion:

> If you combine the psychological and neurological evidence, it is hard to avoid concluding that babies are just plain smarter than we are, at least if being smart means being able to learn something new.

CHAPTER THREE

THE THINGS WHICH I HAVE SEEN

An Interlude about Painting

In his book *Impro* Keith Johnstone describes his first art lesson at his training college, given by Anthony Stirling. The students were told to mix up thick, jammy black paint, and to make on the paper the marks left by a clown riding on and off it on a one-wheeled bicycle. Duly the students covered their paper with a mess of black tracks. Then they had to put colours in the shapes the clown had made. "What colours?" they asked, and were told to choose whatever colours they liked. They obeyed reluctantly and soon everyone's paper was a soggy mess, but Stirling added to the confusion by telling them to put patterns on the colours. "What sort of patterns?" they asked, and were told to draw whatever patterns they felt like. Glumly they daubed on, and when they had all finished Stirling went to a cupboard and brought out an armful of paintings, which he spread on the floor.

Johnstone goes on:

It was the same exercise done by other students. The colours were so beautiful, the patterns so inventive – clearly they had been done by some advanced class. 'What a great idea,' I thought, 'making us screw up in this way and then letting us realise that there was something better we could learn, since the advanced students were so much better.' Maybe I exaggerate when I remember how beautiful the paintings were, but I was seeing them immediately after my failure. Then I noticed that these little masterpieces were signed in very scrawly writing. 'Wait a minute,' I said, 'these are by young children!' They were all by eight-year-olds! It was just an exercise to make them use the whole area of the paper, but they'd done it with such love and care and sensitivity. I was speechless. Something happened to me in that moment from which I have never recovered. It was the final confirmation that my education had been a destructive process.

The transition between the eight-year-old who loves colour and the student who wants to conform is echoed in other areas, and generally speaking it is the teachers who engineer the deterioration. In another passage Johnstone describes how, when he was eighteen, he was astonished to find himself weeping over a book. "If I'd wept over a poem in the classroom," he says, "the teacher would have been appalled. I realised that my school had been teaching me *not* to respond."

If we were lucky, when we were older we may have been encouraged to respond again. I remember how impressed I was hearing a lecturer at Cambridge who wept and analysed simultaneously. He was reading a poem by Baudelaire. "Et mon coeur, comme un bloc rouge et glacé," he read with wet eyes. "You get the contrast there, rouge – et glacé." I remember it and I was impressed by it but at the age of twenty-one I used the anecdote as a joke to amuse people at parties. In my world it was not done to show emotion, and probably we felt it was somewhat shameful even to feel emotion. We changed, or some of us did, but it was too late. When, a few years later, a friend told me that he had been moved to tears by an exhibition of paintings by Samuel Palmer I was envious that such a thing was possible.

Memories of Moral Awareness

It is not only aesthetic responses that are hampered by adult interference. It is also basic moral assumptions. I remember my own desperate determination always to tell the truth, and my reluctance to humiliate any adult by beating them in a game. These attitudes resulted in some curious behaviour; I once reported myself for talking in the dormitory after lights out, and playing cards with my mother I had sometimes to face the terrible dilemma of whether to win, or to cheat — which was another despicable action — in order to avoid winning.

As I write these words I find it necessary to adopt a mocking tone as a form of self-defence. If I were writing of the time I ran away, or the times when my friends and I hid so that they could not be taken home, or the times when I made the adults caring for me cry, then I would not feel the same anxiety about being taken for an imbecile. I committed another act of shameful benevolence at school at the age of nine, when we were each supposed to be checking our neighbour's answers to some test; instead of putting ticks by the right answers and crosses by the wrong ones, I corrected his mistakes and ticked them all.

I wept when I read Oscar Wilde's fairy tales, particularly *The Nightingale and the Rose* and *The Happy Prince* because the birds suffered as a result of their efforts to do good. My mother had a book of children's songs in which the story of the Babes in the Wood had been blacked out with thick lines of ink because, when she sang it to us, my sister and I had been so distressed. I do not remember the occasion of the singing, but I remember the blacked-out verses and the explanation. It is extremely difficult to confess to virtue. It is not surprising that most people writing of their own lives prefer to make themselves out to be hard.

I still remember my distress over the Oscar Wilde stories, and it was of quite a different order to the deepest reactions to works of art that I have had more recently. In the last ten years or so I have been moved to tears by *Othello*, and, rather surprisingly, by *Candida*, but the experiences were trivial compared with my childhood grief. We train ourselves to withstand emotion. Part of growing up is learning not to cry over fairy-tales, but in learning not to care too much about the fate of characters in fiction we diminish its power to move us. What is worse is that we also learn a certain indifference to the sufferings of real people.

I quote my own comparatively trivial memories of moral dilemmas in the hope of prompting similar memories in the reader. As a much stronger example of the vigour of a child's morals, still in the hope of encouraging recognition rather than making a logical argument, let me quote Eric Gill again.

I remember when I first became aware of the possibility of absolute and irreparable injustice. My mother accused me of doing something I had not done. I forget what it was. It was a trivial matter, but the downright monstrosity of the situation, as such and in itself, gave me even at the time, and perhaps more so then because such a possibility had not previously occurred to me, a real shock... This event did not cause me much pain, moreover the affair was so small I wasn't even punished for it, but it made me think; it seemed so incredible, so impossible, so mentally horrible.

Notice the number of absolutes in his description – the word "absolute" itself, "irreparable", "incredible", "impossible" – and the phrases "downright monstrosity" and "mentally horrible." It is partly the overwhelming nature of moral demands that makes us so eager to limit them and control them as we get older.

More serious dilemmas give rise to greater moral behaviour. Maya Angelou gives an example of heroism on the part of her brother and absolute trust on her own part in an account of what happened between them in hospital after she had been raped by her mother's lover.

In the hospital, Bailey told me that I had to tell who did that to me, or the man would hurt another little girl. When I explained that I couldn't tell because the man would kill him, Bailey said knowingly 'He can't kill me. I won't let him.' And of course I believed him. Bailey didn't lie to me. So I told him.

When this took place Maya Angelou was eight, and her brother Bailey was nine. When the case came to court she was asked whether the man had touched her before. After a pause the question was repeated. She said no because she thought her family would be furious if they knew that before the rape she had found some comfort in what she believed to be the man's affection, and because the man himself looked at her and willed her to say no. "The lie," she says, "lumped in my throat, and I couldn't get air. How I despised the man for making me lie... I could feel the evilness flowing through my body and waiting, pent up, to rush off my tongue if I tried to open my mouth. I clamped my teeth shut, I'd hold it in. If it escaped, wouldn't it flood the world and all the innocent people?"

For nearly a year afterwards she didn't speak at all.

Differences

Children are aware of the differences between their own moral principles and those of the adults around them.

"It was the same old quandary. I had always lived it. There was an army of adults, whose motives and movements I just couldn't understand, and who made no effort to understand mine," wrote Maya Angelou of herself at the age of eight.

Gwen Raverat, in her secure middle-class home, had the same old quandary too.

> Prayer was not the only idea of the grown-ups that seemed to me wrong in itself. They had a complete set of values for Badness and Goodness, which I will call System A; and this only partly coincided with my own private set of values, System B. I was always troubled by the confusion of trying to reconcile the two incompatible codes. System A and System B overlapped and agreed in disapproving of dishonesty, cruelty and cowardliness; but otherwise they had little in common... Obedience, though important in System A, had no place at all in System B.

This question of the importance of obedience is a fundamental one. I shall have more to say about it later.

In Sheila and Celia Kitzinger's book *Talking with Children about Things that Really Matter*, there are accounts of children's moral actions from an adult point of view. The behaviour of children who are dying in hospital is often extremely moving.

According to another doctor (Edmund Pellegrino) many children ask their doctor whether they are dying long before their parents consider telling them, and the child's first concern is, ironically, often to conceal this from her parents, 'so as not to worry them' and 'because I don't want to be a nuisance.' Many children express concern about the time and money spent on them, and feel guilt and ashamed about the grief they are causing their parents. They hope that by concealing the fact that they are dying from them they can spare them some grief.

This reversal of the adult view of the situation, in which it is the child that has to be protected, shows how adults often underestimate their own children, and how much more rewarding their relationship could be if they were able to appreciate their children as they really are.

I hope I have given enough examples to show that children often set themselves extraordinarily high standards. The usual adult response to a child's high moral demands is illustrated in this passage by Osbert Sitwell, about his sister Edith.

> As she grew older, instead of allowing her to find her own range, in the same manner that she had taught herself to read, they tried to force her to comply to their own measurements. Her seriousness, and an attitude of criticism which gradually developed in her concerning current class beliefs (such as that the poor deserved to be poor, the rich, rich, or that sport was of more value to life than art) terrified my mother.

Even if it is used slightly facetiously, "terrified" is an extraordinarily strong word in this context. The other quotations I have used described children's attitudes; this is a description of an adult reaction. Why should an adult be terrified by a child's moral views? If she is wrong, surely the child can simply be corrected. The source of terror for the Sitwells' mother, was, I suggest, that she knew Edith was right. She was not terrified for Edith's sake, she was terrified that she herself might be obliged to reject the whole structure of her social world. In order to grow up an acceptable member of this society, the child would have to abandon many of her accurate moral perceptions.

Talking with Children about Things that Really Matter gives another example of a way in which a child's moral concern can outmatch an adult's.

> Another woman said that 5-year-old Stephanie 'cried and cried about the starving babies in Ethiopia – she was inconsolable for a while, until I thought to suggest helping by sending her pocket money, and she has done this for some weeks now.' Wanting to help by giving toys or money is a common response even in these very young children.

We adults, who are capable of so much more, may perhaps give toys or money, but we have schooled ourselves to be sufficiently indifferent to avoid the inconvenience of continual tears.

There is one more passage I wish to quote before going on to my next chapter, in which I shall look again at what psychologists have to say.

Rian Malan was the son of a right-wing Afrikaner family. He was a descendant of Daniel François Malan, South Africa's first nationalist prime minister who was one of the founders of the apartheid system. This is how he felt about black people when he was very young.

> I loved them all, indiscriminately: Lena, Johannes, Piet, James, Betty, Miriam, Miriam's children and teeming grandchildren, the other Piet, who worked next door, the waiters in the hotel down the road, John's boys – all of them. Loving natives was a very good investment. I learned that at the very beginning, and it remains true to this day. If you were friendly, they lit up and laughed and returned your love a hundredfold. It seemed so ordinary and so easy to love them. Maybe we are all that way in the beginning. Maybe we just grow out of it, or are taught otherwise.

I think Rian Malan is right, but it is not just black people who are easy to love, it is anyone who responds to your affection with love and laughter. To a small child it is so ordinary and so easy to love people. We are all that way in the beginning. Unfortunately we grow out of it, and we are taught otherwise.

CHAPTER FOUR

A SOMEWHAT MORE OBJECTIVE CHAPTER

Old Perceptions of Children's Abilities

There are two criticisms to be made of the argument so far. One is that it is shamefully unscientific to base an argument on a few subjective accounts and an appeal to the reader's sympathy. The second is that personal memories can offer no reliable description of the very first years of life because hardly anyone remembers them. Of course I am not pretending to write a scientific book, but a little can be done to answer both criticisms by reference to the research that has been done into the moral development of children.

Ever since Piaget propounded his theories of stages of intellectual development, other research has been lowering the ages at which the stages are reached. He based most of his research on experiments rather than on observation of children in their everyday life, and usually depended on children's verbal responses to questions. It was this that misled him. One example will be enough to demonstrate what went wrong. The researcher showed the child a bunch of flowers, five of which were red and three yellow, and asked "Are there more red flowers or more yellow flowers?" The child naturally answered correctly, and was then asked, "Are there more red flowers, or more flowers?" Young children would answer this second question wrongly, but this would not have been, as Piaget thought, because they did not understand the question at all, but because they answered a different one. The problem was expressed in such a ridiculous way that they naturally completed the apparently unfinished sentence and answered the far more reasonable question – "Are there more red flowers, or more flowers of other colours?" The normal way of asking the question Piaget wanted asked is simply "Are all the flowers red?" It is arguable that the children's supposedly wrong answers were the most sensible response possible to a virtually nonsensical question.

(For thoroughly satisfying demolition of the basic assumptions behind Piaget's experiments with children's concepts of quantity, I recommend chapter four of Gareth B. Matthews' book, *The Philosophy of Childhood*.)

Research into Moral Development

The same pattern has arisen in the study of moral development. Moral characteristics, thought at one time to emerge during late childhood and adolescence, have been observed at earlier and earlier ages.

Piaget's own research in this area, a large part of which involved asking about twenty boys aged between four and thirteen how to play marbles, seems out of date. Quite apart from the artificiality and triviality of the experiment, it is largely a test of the boys' articulacy, and even Piaget made no attempt to use it with children younger than four, nor with girls. Boys younger than four were apparently not thought to have started developing morally just yet, and girls were not even worth considering. The part of Piaget's research that did not involve marbles consisted of asking his subjects to assess the behaviour of children in stories involving lying, stealing and *clumsiness*. I don't think there can be many people in western society who still regard clumsiness as a moral issue.

C. W. Valentine, in *The Normal Child*, published in 1956, thought it relevant to say that Cyril Burt, in devising mental tests, set defining kindness, charity and justice as tasks for fourteen-year-olds, and that even at fourteen the definitions most children produced were fairly weak. However, he went on to say that "About the age of 9 or 10 a few general concepts as to right and wrong appear."

Valentine was sadly out of date. Peck and Havighurst had done some much more important research than Piaget's with a group of 120 children who were born in a small town in the Midwest of the United States in 1933, and who were still living there ten years later. They too used tests which depended on the children's articulacy to some extent, but the tests were more varied than Piaget's and included sentence completion and the interpretation of pictures showing ambiguous social situations; the researchers also consulted the children's teachers, and when they narrowed down the group to what was considered to be a manageable but nevertheless typical 34, they also interviewed the children and got to know them well.

Peck and Havighurst found five types of moral behaviour: amoral, when you seek only direct personal gratification; expedient, when moral behaviour occurs because you perceive some consequent advantage; conforming, when all that matters is not to stand out from the crowd; irrational-conscientious, when you have accepted some moral code and stand by it however absurd it may be; and rational-altruistic, when you are concerned for the welfare of others and take proper measures to achieve it. The first two types – amoral and expedient – were thought to be consecutive stages of development occurring in infancy and early childhood, the next two – conforming and irrational-conscientious – were thought to be parallel stages appropriate in later childhood, and to be stages where most people stopped advancing, and the final type – rational-altruistic – was thought to be rare.

By the 1960s these types of behaviour were still broadly accepted, but they were no longer seen as consecutive stages. Adults were considered to be influenced by all five types of moral consideration, often indeed by several of them at any one time, and Norman Williams' analysis of the research sponsored by the Farmington Trust in the late 1960s found evidence of all five types in the youngest children involved in the study, who were four. This research, though, also depended on the children's articulacy. A standard interview was devised so that it could be used with a large sample – in fact 790 children were interviewed. They were asked about the meaning of such concepts as lying, fairness or bullying, and were then asked whether such actions were right or wrong, and why they were right or wrong. It is not surprising that the researchers decided on a minimum age of four.

In 1969 Lawrence Kohlberg redefined the stages of moral development, and found six stages, divided into three groups of two – pre-conventional, conventional and post-conventional – the first two of which correspond broadly to Peck and Havighurst's stages expedient and conformist. The third group, though rational, does not correspond to the stage rational-altruistic; people who have reached this level relate moral decisions to absolute standards rather than to the conventions of society, but they do not have to show consideration for other people. Kohlberg considered morality to be something that could only be appreciated intellectually, a system of rules based on the distribution of rights and duties according to principles of equality and reciprocity. It was not until the publication of *Friendship, Altruism and Morality* by Lawrence Blum in 1980 that the idea that altruistic emotion could actually be a more effective guide to behaviour than any rigid intellectual system began to be taken seriously. At about the same time Carol Gilligan, who was collaborating with Kohlberg in some of his research, began to notice that women discussed moral questions in a different way from men. This led her to new perceptions, and her important book, *In a Different Voice*, was published in 1982.

In a Different Voice

Carol Gilligan was at that time Professor of Education at Harvard Graduate School of Education. She found the reason for the absence of the feminine morality when she looked again at earlier research.

In Piaget's account of the moral judgment of the child, published in 1932, girls are an aside, a curiosity to whom he devotes four brief entries in an index that omits "boys" altogether because "the child" is assumed to be male; in the research from which Kohlberg derives his theory, females simply do not exist. Kohlberg's six stages that describe the development of moral judgment from childhood to adulthood were based on the study of eighty-four boys. He did not include any girls at all.

Gilligan distinguished two approaches to moral questions that she called the justice approach and the caring approach. Kohlberg had been concerned solely with the justice approach, which is typically male. Gilligan was concerned with both approaches, and found that the caring approach, ignored by Kohlberg, was the more important approach for women.

The descriptive terms are clear. The justice approach is based on fairness, personal rights, rules and set standards of behaviour; individual welfare is a secondary consideration. The caring approach is a concern for the welfare of other people, regardless of rules.

Gilligan and the others working with her have found over and over again that, though neither sex is limited to one type of response, males are more likely to make justice responses and females are more likely to make caring responses.

Children, too, are more likely to make caring responses than justice responses. Kohlberg's analysis of what he saw as the moral development of boys was actually an analysis of their movement from a care-based morality to a rule-based morality, and I see this as not a development but a decline.

Peck and Havighurst's five descriptions of moral behaviour, on the other hand, remain useful as long as it is realised that they are not stages of development. Their highest category, rational altruism, is clearly an aspect of a morality of care.

Moral Discussions with Five-Year-Olds

Vivian Gussin Paley, who taught at the Laboratory Schools of the University of Chicago, tape-recorded young children's conversations in her classroom. She has published a number of books of transcriptions of these recordings, together with comments and examples of the stories the children dictated to her. An extract from *Wally's Stories* illustrates the moral thinking of five-year-olds.

Jill: Every time I listen to the Ella Jenkins record, you know it's supposed to say "Yes ma'am" but Tanya says "No ma'am" louder and louder.

Tanya: So does Wally.

Wally:	I only did it once.
Jill:	Tanya *keeps keeps* doing it.
Teacher:	You told her to stop?
Jill:	I *keep keep* telling her. The next time she comes in and I put on that record I'm going to just take it off.
Teacher:	Why do that? There should be a rule about bothering people when they're listening to records.
Jill:	Next time Tanya comes in I'm going to leave.
Teacher:	Why should you be the one to leave?
Jill:	So she won't bother me.
Deana:	Here's a good rule: if you want to fool around, don't sing with a record.
Wally:	Whoever says "No ma'am" has to say "Yes ma'am".
Mickey:	Keep changing the record until you find one Tanya likes.
Teacher:	Is that fair to Jill?
Mickey:	Sure. Jill could listen to the different record too.
Teacher:	Tanya, it seems to me you should leave if you spoil the record, but they don't agree with me.
Tanya:	If I do it again I'll just take a book until I stop saying "No ma'am."
Jill:	Or maybe I'll just put on a record you like.

The previous day I had made Tanya leave the art table after she splattered paint on Ellen's picture. Tanya shouted, "I'm never going to paint again!" After lunch she returned to the painting table and repeated her mischief. Lisa looked up and said, "Tanya's just jealous."

In the record corner the children said: we like you, Tanya, and you can stay. They did not withhold friendship or impose hardships, and Tanya had stopped teasing. I had excluded Tanya from the art table and achieved little besides temporary peace and quiet.

Eddie breaks a clay house made by Earl. It is obvious he has done it on purpose.

Teacher:	Why did you do that, Eddie? That was not nice!
Lisa:	He has to make Earl another house.
Warren:	Don't let him play with clay for two days.
Wally:	Let him pick his own punishment. Okay, Eddie?
Eddie:	I'm not picking a punishment and I don't care if I ever play with clay. And I didn't know it was Earl's house.
Teacher:	Well, it had to be someone's house, didn't it?
Tanya:	Let Eddie invite Earl to his house and Earl can decide everything they do all day long.
Fred:	Let Earl break something of Eddie's.
Teacher:	Which idea sounds fair, Earl?
Earl:	That Eddie make me a new house.
Eddie:	I don't want to.
Wally:	Okay. Let someone else do it.
Fred:	I'll do it!
Earl:	Fred can do it.
Teacher:	How about Eddie?
Earl:	He'll do it some other time.
Wally:	Here's something really not fair. Deana and Jill always pick the very same people to act in their stories. They never pick me.
Teacher:	But they write the story. Can't they pick the actors?
Everyone:	No!
Ellen:	Then people just feel bad. You have to pick someone who didn't have a turn.
Wally:	I only got one turn. In my own story.
Deana:	I only got four turns.
Andy:	I never had a turn!
Tanya:	Yes, you did too. You were the lion in my story.
Wally:	He was a wolf. I was the lion.
Teacher:	How can we remember who had turns?

Deana:	Go cubby by cubby – like for leaders.
Wally:	Start with my cubby because I'm down by the door.
Deana:	Start with Rose because she never writes a story.
Wally:	Okay, start with Rose.

They worry about Rose, who never writes stories and therefore never gets first choice of roles. Tanya feels left out in the record corner, so they look for a record she will like. Eddie can make up for his transgressions at another time when he's in a better mood. Fairness is given a high priority in the kindergarten.

Vivian Gussin Paley listens to her children with extraordinary attention, but I don't think it is fairness that concerns the children, I think it is happiness. Tanya is unhappy and needs a special concession. Earl's house has been destroyed, but he will be happy again as long as he has another house, and Fred will make one for him, so there is no need to impose any unpleasantness on Eddie, who is already cross about something. Rose will be happier if she has turns acting stories. If people don't get turns then they feel bad. Fairness, generally speaking, helps to make people happy, but it is not important in itself. It is not strictly speaking fair that Fred should make a new house for Earl when it was Eddie who broke the old one, but it makes everyone happy so it is a more sensible solution to the problem than a strictly fair one.

In these children's minds happiness is more important than justice, but it is not their own happiness they are concerned about, it is the happiness of other people. This is clearly rational altruism. The teacher has tried to introduce a justice-based morality, but the children have insisted on a morality of caring.

Observations in the Home

Vivan Gussin Paley is a teacher and not a psychologist, but by the 1980s psychological research had moved on too, from asking children difficult abstract questions to observing them in their own families, and the results were very different. Professor Judith Dunn's research in Cambridge, described in her book *The Beginnings of Social Understanding*, dealt only with children up to the age of three, amoral in Peck and Havighurst's opinion, and according to Piaget at best egocentric but principally at the motor stage, acting without any deliberate purpose at all. Professor Dunn had no child-centred line she was seeking to justify, indeed rather the contrary; she refers to babies learning especially fast when they can themselves influence what is happening "just as in real life *people* do" (my italics), and at another point she says small children are facing the task of "becoming human". She came to the subject of her research while she was working on a different topic which involved long observations in the children's own homes; she noticed apparent powers of understanding in young children that were well in advance of what she had been led to expect, and therefore decided to study their development in a systematic manner to find out whether her impressions were justified.

They were. From the age of eighteen months children know how to hurt, and how to comfort, and how to make the distress worse; they understand something of what is allowed and not allowed within their families and anticipate adults' responses to their own misdeeds and to the misdeeds of others; they categorise these misdeeds; they ask about the causes of other people's behaviour; they respond to other people's distress; they make jokes. By the time they are three they have some idea of responsibility, of how to make excuses or justify something they have done and they begin to comment on the morality of other people's behaviour. Small children obviously do not behave with absolute moral rectitude, any more than anyone else does, but even very young children are interested in moral issues and they are learning about them all the time, particularly rapidly when they themselves are emotionally involved in the situation. They are not necessarily able to discuss their feelings – at eighteen months they are certainly not able to – but they are able to make them manifest. Karen Wynn of MIT has shown that children have an implicit idea of number before they even learn to speak; in a similar way they seem to have implicit moral understanding before they are able to express it.

Professor Dunn quotes Lawrence Blum's essay *Particularity and Responsiveness* in support of her view that by the age of three a child has good foundations for caring, considerateness and kindness, and M. J. Parker's paper delivered in 1986, which says that even two- and three-year-olds, when they meet situations where others are in conflict or distress, have ways of coping with them. This effective concern for the distress of others can surely be described as altruistic emotion.

Unless we refuse to believe Professor Dunn it seems that all Peck and Havighurst's types of moral approach are present even before the age of two. The children's understanding and experience are limited, but their concern for others is self-evident. And even their understanding, at least of the family situation as it concerns them, is enormously greater than was thought twenty or thirty years ago.

In 1992 a prominent team of psychologists conducted research into prosocial behaviour in infants aged fourteen months (R. N. Emde et al.). The experts continue to recognise moral responses in younger and younger children.

A Question

Discussions of psychological research usually end with fresh questions. The question that interests me is "When does moral sensitivity start to decline?" The development of moral sensitivity in children is being investigated all the time, but there seems to be an assumption that after a certain point we become morally mature human beings and stop changing, in much the same way as we stop growing physically. What I should like someone to investigate is the moral equivalent of baldness, the menopause and middle-aged spread.

CHAPTER FIVE

WHERE IS IT NOW?

Whither is fled the visionary gleam?
Where is it now, the glory and the dream?

William Wordsworth

Distortion of Religion

In Chapter Three I gave examples to show that children are clearly capable of deep moral feelings and understand concepts of right and wrong without needing instruction. In Chapter Four I quoted evidence in support of this view from psychological research. In this chapter I shall discuss what happens to extinguish this moral vision.

The answer, I am afraid, is moral instruction.

There is usually enormous hypocrisy involved in the way this instruction is carried out. Instead of saying, "We know you know what is right, but we have not the moral strength to act like that. We do our best. We make compromises," the adult world presents itself as infallible.

One of the tools that can be used for this deceit is religion. I actually heard a sermon delivered to boys at Repton School, in which the preacher began with his text – "Go, and sell that thou hast, and give to the poor" – and immediately said "This of course does not mean that we should sell what we have and give the money to the poor." We have been taught to accept this sort of moral dishonesty as normal.

I do not suppose that Margaret Thatcher was deliberately misusing Christian ideas when she addressed the General Assembly of the Church of Scotland in 1988, but her talk gave several examples of the same kind of distortion of moral values. She even succeeded in twisting Christ's recommendation, "Love thy neighbour as thyself," to make it justify hatred. She confessed that she had always had difficulty with understanding the precept until she found help from C. S. Lewis: "He pointed out that we don't exactly love ourselves," she said, "when we fall far below the standards and beliefs we have accepted. Indeed we might even hate ourselves for some unworthy deed." So it is right to hate our neighbours when they are unworthy, and the criteria by which they are to be judged unworthy are the standards and beliefs we, not they, have accepted.

This was an address to the General Assembly of the Church of Scotland, not a talk in a school assembly, but it was full of evasions of the moral point. "The Tenth Commandment – Thou shalt not covet – recognises that making money and owning things could become selfish activities. But it is not the creation of wealth that is wrong, but the love of money for its own sake." Margaret Thatcher said "could become" when she ought to have said "are". In the next sentence she used the phrase "the creation of wealth" and failed to distinguish between the wealth of the community and the wealth of the individual. As the owner of nine and a half million pounds (in 1992), she needed to nudge aside moral criticism.

Her main excuse for her blatantly plutocratic principles was one that is also used by many other people, often including the clergy: "We must recognise that modern society is infinitely more complex than that of Biblical times and of course new occasions teach new duties." In other words, we can be good Christians even if we don't stick to the old moral standards; it is quite all right to invent less demanding ones of our own.

When religion is used to persuade children to escape from the simple questions of right and wrong that they understand so thoroughly, they are usually led through two stages. The first stage presents a religious authority for a moral code that closely resembles the children's natural view, and when obedience to a code has taken the place of reliance on personal conscience, then the second stage adapts and twists the code and finally replaces it with a new one that is somehow supposed to be more relevant or more up to date.

All that this suggests is that the child who is enchanted by religion is likely to be misled. The psychiatrist Alice Miller suggests a worse fate. In *For Your Own Good*, published in 1983, she reports that "60% of German terrorists in recent years have been the children of protestant clergy." A dogmatic and authoritarian upbringing, she believes, prevents children from ever making any contact with their true selves, and when they become adults this leads them to pass on to other people the intolerance and violence they experienced in their childhood.

Dubious Virtues 1: Obedience

There is little to be said for the idea of obedience.

Gwen Raverat mentioned it as a virtue that was part of the adult code but not of her own. Even from the simplest practical point of view obedience is a highly dubious virtue. Who are we to obey?

For those in authority, the answer is obvious – "You are to obey us." That is why parents approve of obedience, and teachers approve of obedience, and policemen and judges and governments. Unless they are obeyed, society falls apart, they believe.

From the point of view of the children, or anyone else who is supposed to do the obeying, the question is a great deal more difficult. Are we always to do whatever anyone tells us to do? The question is obviously absurd. Was Rian Malan supposed to obey the rightwing Afrikaners? Was the man who raped the eight-year-old Maya Angelou entitled to make her obey him? Obedience is a concept invented by those in authority to make it easier to achieve their own ends, to relieve them of the tasks of persuasion and justification. It is a description of a certain type of behaviour, but it is not a virtue. If there is a moral question involved in the concept of obedience, it is the question of deciding who to obey. Even if an answer can be found to that question, it seems almost certain that obedience weakens moral judgement rather than strengthening it. Children who obey do not have to decide, and they may well be robbed of confidence in their own innate judgement.

In the late sixties and early seventies the American psychologist Ervin Staub conducted experiments that are relevant to this point. Children were asked to wait in a room by themselves. They would hear the sound of a falling chair in the next room, followed by crying and moaning from a young girl. After the age of eight or nine, the older the children were the less likely they were to go to see whether they could help. By thirteen they were less likely to try to help than nursery school children. When they were asked about it afterwards they said they were afraid of being told off by the researcher if they disobeyed him and left the room.

Dubious Virtues 2: Conformity

A part of our childish insight may be taken from us by religion, and a part of it by obedience, but a far more powerful moderator of behaviour is the desire to conform. When I first went to boarding school at the age of eight I found that my ideas were so often out of line with the accepted views that people used to laugh at me. After a while I learned to take advantage of this, and acquired a reputation for being funny. It was a way of avoiding conformity, and it earned me a certain popularity, but it cost me all my dignity and much of my self-respect. I still remember going into a class-room when I was fourteen or so and being greeted by two of the more alarming of my fellow-pupils. "Here's Gribble," they said. "He's mad." I had no defence.

Gareth B. Matthews, in *The Philosophy of Childhood*, gives many examples of children's philosophical remarks that stand out uncomfortably in ordinary conversation, remarks such as "All the world is made of colours," or "How can we be sure that everything is not a dream?" or "The only thing that goes on for ever and ever is numbers." He says:

My informal research suggests that... spontaneous excursions into philosophy are not at all unusual for children between the ages of three and seven; in somewhat older children, though, even eight- and nine-year-olds, they become rare, or at least rarely reported. My hypothesis is that, once children become well settled into school, they learn that only "useful" questioning is expected of them. Philosophy then either goes underground, to be pursued privately, perhaps, and not shared with others, or else becomes totally dormant.

I found this view confirmed in 2004 when I visited Caol Primary School, the home of the amazing Room 13 art room.[2] Rob Fairley, the artist in residence employed by the children, told me that he started teaching pure philosophy in a fairly formal way to seven- and eight-year-olds, but found that two years on they didn't understand what he was saying. Then when they were eleven or twelve the interest would re-awaken.

Lynne Smith, the teacher of the year sevens, used to present her class with five big questions:

What happens to the part of you that is you when you die?

What is beyond space?

How did the universe begin?

When and how will the world end?

Why are we here?

The children would discuss these issues with enthusiasm, encouraged by her admission that she did not know the answers herself, and produce a wide variety of responses. Then one year she asked her class how many of them had already thought about these questions earlier. Most of them had. And how many of them had ever talked about their ideas with other people? Hardly any of them.

It is safer not to expose your deepest thoughts. No matter how fascinating your efforts to understand the world about you, no matter how much work adult philosophers have put into dealing with problems such as yours, it is safer to be "useful", to conform.

---

2   See Chapter Sixteen.

Conforming with a group means you lose part of your individuality, but you gain acceptance among your peers. It is at least as important to adults as it is to children, and I may make its shortcomings clearer by describing the mature, adult form, rather than the simpler conformity demanded in childhood. Among adults, drinking pints of beer, piercing your nose and having your arms tattooed wins you status in one group, drinking only obscure brands of whisky, patronising shop-assistants and using embossed writing-paper in another. These purely external but often very wide-ranging methods of self-identification usually also entail certain political or social opinions, and nearly always involve scorn for anyone who does not belong to the group. Conformity to the group's standards seems a good deal more important than sticking to one's own moral principles. Most of us do not have enough confidence in our own judgement to stand up against public opinion, and curiously we gain a stronger impression of personal worth from being part of a group or social class with whom we have a certain amount in common than we do from standing to one side as individuals.

For this reason we tend to emphasise our similarities to others and play down our idiosyncrasies unless they happen to be amusing or generally accepted. What is accepted is often in moral terms highly undesirable – drinking too much, for instance, or driving too fast, or sexual promiscuity, or a baseless assumption of superiority.

The snob, who relies entirely on class distinctions for his judgement of other people, will turn a blind eye to any of these faults, but what he will not turn a blind eye to is excessive self-sacrifice. It is a bit dubious to work in an Oxfam shop or cut down your use of the car to avoid pollution, but it is beyond the pale to question the accepted values by, for instance, advocating the general redistribution of wealth. Charles Moore, at the time editor of the Daily Telegraph, put this view succinctly: "As for the people who say they are happy to pay extra taxes in order to ensure that we live in a more civilised society, I am afraid I want to punch them on the nose."

This is the kind of attitude society seems to want children to learn. In spite of its patent moral irrelevance, conformity somehow manages to take on the authority of a moral point of view. "Wrong" is used to describe offences against conventions. "He wears the wrong kind of trainers," an adolescent might say, as a strong condemnation. "Mary knows all the wrong people," sneers an older person, in fact only meaning that Mary knows people who do not belong to the speaker's own approved group.

Conformity is superficially a good deal more comfortable than morality. None of us is any too keen on selling what we have and giving to the poor. It is much easier to drop the odd pound into the charity box and wear the right sweatshirts.

A child learns to conform by observing society. Refusing to conform for moral reasons is extremely difficult. Parents try to prevent any such behaviour. "Don't be so silly," they say. "What will people think if you do that?" They understand the risk of becoming an outcast, but they do not understand the cost to the children of not being true to themselves.

Poisonous Pedagogy

In *For Your Own Good* Alice Miller describes the nineteenth-century methods of bringing up children, which she calls "poisonous pedagogy." Her summary shows that all too much of it is still widely practised.

The methods that can be used to suppress vital spontaneity in the child are: laying traps, lying, duplicity, subterfuge, manipulation, "scare" tactics, withdrawal of love, isolation, distrust, humiliating and disgracing the child, scorn, ridicule, and coercion even to the point of torture.

It is also a part of the "poisonous pedagogy" to impart to the child from the beginning false information and beliefs that have been passed on from generation to generation and dutifully accepted by the young even though they are not only unproven but are demonstrably false. Examples of such beliefs are:

1.   A feeling of duty produces love.

2.   Hatred can be done away with by forbidding it.

3.   Parents deserve respect simply because they are parents.

4.   Children are undeserving of respect simply because they are children.

5.   Obedience makes a child strong.

6.   A high degree of self-esteem is harmful.

7. A low degree of self-esteem makes a person altruistic.

8. Tenderness (doting) is harmful.

9. Responding to a child's needs is wrong.

10. Severity and coldness are a good preparation for life.

11. A pretence of gratitude is better than honest ingratitude.

12. The way you behave is more important than the way you really are.

13. Neither parents nor God would survive being offended.

14. The body is something dirty and disgusting.

15. Strong feelings are harmful.

16. Parents are creatures free of drives and guilt.

17. Parents are always right.

These powerful lists deserve long consideration, but my concern at the moment is only to show how many ways there are in which a child's moral perceptions can be effectively blunted.

Set Your Expectations Low

Idealism, even in adults, is regarded with fierce suspicion. "I can't stand his holier-than-thou attitude," people say. Sometimes they may be objecting fairly enough to a hypocritical show-off, but more often they are simply excusing their embarrassment at finding someone whose values, in some respect or other, are plainly superior to their own. Nevertheless the phrase is strongly derogatory, and most of us go out of our way to avoid suggesting that we are in any way morally superior to anybody at all in whose company we find ourselves. It is thought offensive to reveal that you always declare everything at the customs, or that every time beggars approach you, you give them all your loose cash. If you do such things there is a widespread feeling that you ought to keep quiet about it, because otherwise you are implying a criticism of other people.

In adults such behaviour is considered tiresome, but in children it is treated as laughable. I can see nothing funny in a child trying to insist on an uncle keeping to the speed limit, or objecting to a parent telling lies to avoid an unwanted encounter. The effect of mocking children who express concern about such things is to shake their confidence in their own moral perceptions. They feel they know what is right, but those they love seem to think their views are ridiculous.

One of the first protections most children need to build for themselves is an indifference to adult ridicule. They are laughed at so often for well-intentioned actions that they have to learn to ignore the laughter. As we get older we are less often ridiculous in other people's eyes and we lose this habitual indifference. The older we get the more likely we are to think it is more shameful to be ridiculous than to be wrong. That is one of the reasons why idealists are usually young.

In spite of the evidence, it is not usually admitted that we discard more and more moral principles as we get older. It is thought that as well as getting older, we get wiser. We certainly get more experienced, and for most of our lives we go on getting better at making use of that experience. What seems extremely unlikely is that we go on using that experience for better and better ends. We come to rely more and more on custom and convention rather than on conscience. Nowadays you even meet people who advance financial reasons for moral decisions; someone might say "I didn't want to make a claim against her, but there was a lot of money involved, so it was only right." It is not far from that position to "I had a chance of making a good deal of money out of them, so it was only right." Making money becomes a moral obligation. In her address to the Church of Scotland Mrs. Thatcher seemed to have reached that position in all seriousness.

Hiding Moral Issues

Children have moral standards of their own, but by the time they have grown up they have learnt to keep most of them well concealed. The world as described by Margaret Thatcher has been too strong for them. Obedience, conformity and religious injunctions have taken the place of the individual conscience. If ever a high moral idea struggles to the surface, it is quickly sunk again by ridicule. The principal rule of behaviour is "Do not offend against the accepted code. Be neither better nor worse than anybody else."

This means that moral judgement is not exercised. If lack of exercise were the only problem, it might lead to nothing worse than a decline in the ability to make moral distinctions, just as leaving the intellect idle results in a decrease in intellectual power. Unfortunately it is rather worse than that, because moral judgement is actually repressed; we have trained ourselves to ignore our charitable impulses. It is as if, in the intellectual sphere, we deliberately avoid thinking, and automatically reject any ideas that we are unfortunate enough to find developing in our minds. Under these circumstances you would expect not so much a decline as a collapse.

An example of the adult attitude to children's moral sensitivity will serve to illustrate the skills which we acquire in evading moral issues. The adult world feels that children are easily distressed, and therefore need to be protected from the truth. It is not good for children to know that people are tortured to death in police states, that Europe keeps food mountains while Africa starves, that they themselves can innocently inspire perverse sexual desires and suffer from the consequences. Such things may happen on television screens, but they are not generally discussed at home or at school.

This view leads to adults also protecting themselves from the consideration of such horrifying facts, and consequently prevents them from making any effort to do anything about them. When there is great publicity for a sudden natural disaster money and offers of help come flowing in. The long-term disasters inspire only a sense of despair, and most of us close our eyes in order to avoid sharing in the suffering. "Don't let the children see," we say, and this becomes extremely close in meaning to, "Don't let this trouble my conscience."

Adults, though, have also learnt to do more positive things to protect themselves than merely closing their eyes. The "Yes, but" response is a useful one. "Wouldn't it be a good thing to transport the European food-mountains to places where the food would be eaten?" "Yes, of course, but ..." But what? But it would cost too much money. But the food wouldn't get distributed to the right people. But it would be left to rot on the quayside. But giving food away would damage the local market. But the roads are inadequate. But the regimes are corrupt. But it would be an opportunity for the black market to flourish. Yes, of course, but we don't really want to because we have pressing concerns of our own.

In spite of all our efforts, children still challenge us. They tell us to invite beggars home and feed them. They tell us to stop that man from kicking his dog. They tell us that we and our spouses should drop our quarrels and create a happy home again. They tell us that we should eat less and send the food to Somalia.

Yes, but ...

As people grow older they gain in experience and skill and knowledge, but they also build a wall around their consciences. Children don't obey their consciences all the time, but at least they are aware of them, and are aware of their power. They are not ashamed of being concerned about others. A good deal of our adult mental energy goes, consciously or subconsciously, towards beating down our uncomfortable certainties about right and wrong, disputing them, confusing them, explaining them away and, when they are sufficiently weakened, shutting them behind a wall and ignoring them altogether. Our education has provided us with plenty of methods of suppression.

Part of growing up is learning how to protect yourself from intrusive moral requirements that are actually part of your own personality. Part of growing up is learning how to cripple your own conscience.

Tony Blair's government by spin illustrated this process. He managed to persuade his party to accept the idea that the creation and preservation of wealth was more important than the elimination of poverty and privilege, and he did this by presenting himself as a decent, Christian, honest man and implying that only people who lacked those virtues can oppose his ideas. It was not until his power was beginning to fade that other members of the Labour Party felt strong enough to express contrary opinions. Just as you feel obliged to conform to school rules as a child, so you feel obliged to conform to party rules as a Member of Parliament. Conformity, for the successfully educated, is more important than principle.

In 1842, during the parliamentary debate on the colliery bill, which sought to prevent women and children being forced to work in the mines, Lord Egerton made a speech in which he quoted an unnamed clergyman:

This gentleman states, unwillingly but conscientiously, that he fears that the peculiar bend of the back, and other physical peculiarities requisite to the employment, cannot be obtained if the children are initiated at a later age than twelve.

The moral peculiarity requisite to our present society is a peculiar bend of the conscience, and by the age of twelve most children are well initiated.

In the next chapters I shall describe some situations where children have not been required to demonstrate that peculiar bend of the conscience.

CHAPTER SIX

SANDS SCHOOL

The End of the Great Dartington Hall School

For over thirty years I taught in progressive schools. I taught at Dartington Hall School until it closed in 1987, and immediately two other Dartington teachers and I collaborated with a group of children to set up Sands School, which now operates in Ashburton, Devon. The closing of Dartington is something I still find it impossible to forgive, but it did provide the impetus for the setting up of a new school that was in some respects even more closely in line with children's needs, though it could never match Dartington in terms of facilities and variety of opportunity.

When I first arrived at Dartington in 1959 most important decisions were taken by the moot, an assembly which all the staff and children could attend, and where each person present had a single vote. Soon after my arrival the whole book of rules was scrapped, and replaced by a score of new ones which took only a single side of A4. There was no system of punishment. By the 1980s, rule-making had gradually been taken over by the staff. However, nothing much happened if you broke a rule. The real code of behaviour, instead of being agreed by pupils and staff together, was decided by the pupils alone, and was quite independent of the staff decisions. To a large extent the wishes of the pupils and the expectations of the staff coincided – after all, they had assembled there so that the pupils could acquire an academic education – and the school continued to run happily and successfully until a behaviourist who was head in 1983 for only a single term tried to exercise his personal authority, impose sanctions and eliminate sixty years' tradition of tolerance, understanding and co-operation. His failure and his revenge for his failure, widely reported in every British newspaper throughout the silly season, resulted in the school closing for lack of pupils three years later. Towards the end of those three years an effort was made to revive the system of self-government by instituting a number of management committees of staff and pupils to deal with different aspects of the running of the school, but then a new head was appointed and that was the end.

Sands School

I have been asked over and over again to describe the essence of progressive education in a few words, and after failing over and over again I eventually managed to reduce my ideas to a book (*Considering Children*) which seemed to me to express them fairly succinctly. In this chapter I only wish to discuss one issue, which is self-government, or, as Bryn Purdy of Rowen House School prefers to describe it, shared responsibility. After I had written *Considering Children* I worked at Sands School for five years, and there I saw the ideal carried further than I had thought possible at the time I wrote the book, in a way that now seems to me so logical and ordinary that I am astonished that I lacked faith before.

Sands was determined to avoid a fate like Dartington's. The children, aged between eleven and sixteen, were to be involved in all decisions from the very beginning, so that a conflict between school values and pupils' values could never arise. If behaviour occurred which damaged the community, the community itself was to be responsible for dealing with it. At a very early meeting, when there was a discussion about what school rules might be necessary, it was agreed that on the whole common sense should take the place of rules. This meant that if a teacher objected to behaviour that was not self-evidently anti-social, the teacher could not appeal to a rule but must justify the objection from first principles. In fact such situations arose extremely seldom.

The three teachers who were starting the school – Sybilla Higgs, Sean Bellamy and I – invited the children who wanted to join us to several meetings before the school started, so that nothing was arranged without their approval. We started in September 1987 with twenty-two pupils and three teachers. I was appointed headteacher, because the school needed a head to make contact with the outside world and to make sure that things were running smoothly inside the school, but I was given no authority. The parents of one of the pupils offered us the use of the ground floor of their house until we could find a suitable property. It was agreed that we would tidy up the rooms every evening after school to make the house habitable as a home once again. After two terms we moved to a building in Ashburton, a nearby town. The pupils were consulted about the suitability of the house and garden, and everyone except me thought it was ideal, so we bought it. My objections were soon shown to be unfounded, which was one of the early examples of the importance of not allowing a head teacher to make decisions alone.

The two powers the children most wanted were the power to appoint or dismiss teachers, and the power to admit or reject potential pupils. Both these powers have been used with great responsibility; all decisions are made in the school meeting, where each person present, teacher or pupil, has one vote. Generally the most useful contributions to discussion have come from the children; after a trial lesson they have a better idea of whether a teacher can teach than any mere interviewer can acquire, and children who apply for places are often known to many of the present pupils, who are able to guide the meeting in its attempt to assess the answers to the three relevant questions: Does the child want to come to Sands? Will the child make good use of what is on offer at Sands? Will the child spoil the school for others? It is rare that a pupil is rejected, because Sands is generally generous in its attitudes to others, but there have been occasions when the school has felt that though it might be useful to some child, the cost to the other pupils, or to the school itself, would be too high.

After a few years I suggested to the school meeting that Sands did not really need a head teacher, because all the decisions that a head teacher would normally make were taken by the school meeting. My title was changed to administrator. As administrator my duties were to ensure that all necessary decisions were taken and to see that they were implemented.

Lessons I Had to Learn: Case History 1

All this was much as I had expected – perhaps rather better, but not enormously so. The great lessons I learnt resulted from the children's handling of each other's anti-social behaviour. When Sands started I did not know how far the school meeting was to be trusted in this respect; it is now probably the most important feature of the school. Occasions when someone is brought before the school meeting are rare, but when it happens the level of responsibility and care shown is extraordinarily high.

There were two particular incidents which enlightened me. The first concerned a boy who I shall call Peter. He came to us at the age of twelve after having made a disastrous start at a local comprehensive school. He was rather nervous and not very academic, and had some difficulty in making ordinary social contact – he would talk to you but more for the sake of making a noise than saying anything significant – but his difficulties seemed to be of a kind that often disappears when children come to a school like Sands, and when such difficulties are overcome then often academic difficulties evaporate as well. Unfortunately he had another tendency which the school did not discover when he came for interview: when he considered himself under any kind of threat, he would respond with violence, throwing stones or whatever else might come to hand. He would consider himself to be under threat several times a day, and if no one threatened him unprovoked then he would provoke someone until he got a response. I spent hours talking to him – not really talking with him, because of his peculiar attitude – and he would try to provoke me as well. He was extraordinarily good at doing so, and as soon as I raised my voice or showed any sign of irritation he would smile. This helped me to keep my temper in the end, and we were on the verge of being able to discuss his success or lack of success in infuriating me from a detached, other-person point of view, which I hoped would lead to some proper contact with him.

In my diary I wrote, "Crisis over Peter – opening out, having good half-hours but also lots of very bad ones. Able to talk to me sincerely from time to time but very unable to understand what is happening to him and why. Scared, perhaps, and needing reassurance, but going out of his way to reject it. Quite unable to recognise support from for instance [an older boy], who he says kicks him. Very self-righteous and critical of everybody else – they all steal and lie. But I *think* he wants to stay at Sands, and perhaps that is a way we can get him to conform enough for us to be able to help him."

Then, during a single day, he attacked three different children with three different weapons – a broomstick, a metal metre-ruler and a Stanley-knife. As this came not long after an occasion when he had chased someone with an electric drill (luckily without a bit in it), I felt I had to take decisive action. I arranged an appointment for him at the Child Guidance Clinic, and told him he could not come back to the school until the school meeting had decided what further action to take. (To dispel the impression that I was being extremely irresponsible in allowing him to stay in the school for so long, I should perhaps point out that in spite of the savagery of his choice of weapons, Peter never actually injured anybody, which suggests that in fact he was not really trying to hurt them.)

I called a school meeting as soon as Peter had gone and told them what I had done, and suggested that we should discuss whether we were prepared to allow him to come back. I was astonished by the reaction. It was broadly agreed that Peter had had a raw deal in the school, and that people had not been nice enough to him. This was not a matter of some children accusing others, and saying, "You were not nice enough to him," it was the school as a whole saying, "We were not nice enough to him." If he was treated more carefully and given more attention the school should be able to help him. He should certainly be allowed to come back to the school, and everybody should take more trouble to be friendly towards him. Cynic that I was, I also persuaded the meeting that if things went wrong again in spite of all that, it should be left to me to handle the situation, and if necessary I should tell his parents to take him away from the school. I felt that the children would never reach the point of asking him to leave, and that I ought to accept the responsibility of making such an unpleasant decision as a duty for an adult.

Peter came back in due course, after agreeing that he would attend all his timetabled lessons and that if he felt threatened he would not resort to using weapons or throwing missiles. The other children made great efforts to include him and to take an interest in him but he was unable to accept this support; he could not keep to his agreement, he became a danger to other pupils again and so in the end I did call in his parents and recommend that he should be found a place in a special school. In a school like Sands where children spend a lot of their time away from any adult company it seemed too dangerous to allow him to stay.

At the time I felt I had handled this well. I had certainly given up a great deal of my own time to Peter; although I had taken decisive action on my own initiative I had called a school meeting straight afterwards to tell them what I had done, and I had persuaded the meeting to give me the authority to act on my own again if things should go badly and further action be needed. I was moved by the children's generosity in assuming some of the blame for his behaviour, and their efforts to show him support when he returned after being suspended, but I did not understand how much more they might have done if I had not undercut their authority by assuming so much myself. I did not learn this until I was later placed in a situation of apparent absolute stalemate, to which a school meeting found a solution.

Lessons I Had to Learn: Case History 2

This happened when one day all the petty cash disappeared from the cash box in the office – a whole week's supply. The police from Newton Abbot rang up towards the end of the morning to tell the school that they were holding three of our pupils who had been stopped at the railway station where they were trying to buy tickets. The suspicion of the clerk had been aroused because they asked first for tickets to York, and then, when that proved too expensive, they asked for tickets to Brighton. They also had a surprisingly large amount of money for thirteen-year-olds. At the police station they were being extremely uncooperative, but they had given the name of the school so would someone please come and fetch them. We should know that they were also in possession of the spoils of a small shop-lifting raid.

I went to the police station, apologised to the police for their behaviour and was relieved to find that the children were sufficiently eager to get away from the police to come willingly to my car. All three got into the back and we drove out of the town to a lay-by, where I stopped to talk to them.

They were three spitting, swearing bundles of obscene hatred. Sands is a day school, so they were not so much running away from Sands as running away from home. Nevertheless, they had stolen the money from Sands, they hated Sands, they hated the other children, they hated their parents, they hated the school staff, they themselves were the only three people in the world worth knowing, they wanted to know why they couldn't fucking well do whatever they liked and they had intended to go to Brighton and break into a holiday house and live there until their money ran out. Nothing I could think of to say had the slightest effect on them. They seemed absolutely determined to isolate themselves from any sort of sympathy or support.

Without the least idea as to what I should do, I drove them back to school, where they spoke to two other teachers in a similar vein and then announced that they would call a school meeting so that they could tell everybody what had happened and not have it spread about inaccurately by gossip. "We don't want you telling a lot of fucking lies about us," they said. The whole school was by now aware that something unusual had been going on, and everyone attended the meeting.

When the room was quiet the leader of the group quickly, clearly and indifferently told the school exactly what they had done and asked whether the meeting wanted to expel them. At first the other children did not believe it. It did not seem possible that anyone could behave like that and then come in front of a group of people and recount it without any indication of shame or regret. When they realised it was true they were at first so shocked by the apparent lightness with which the story had been told that there threatened to be some confrontation, but Sean Bellamy (the teacher who later took my place as administrator) suggested that that would not be a useful way forward, and from then on the staff hardly spoke at all. The children spoke seriously and wisely and kindly for about an hour. Three who had themselves been in trouble, either at Sands or at previous schools, spoke particularly strongly about the help the school could give them. Two of them were on the edge of tears. "This school is the only one that gives you such love and support," said one girl who was often too self-conscious to express her views. "I know it sounds sentimental but its true." The group were asked whether they wanted to be expelled, or would rather remain at Sands. It seemed they would rather remain.

At the end of the meeting Sean asked, as the absconding children had suggested, for a vote as to whether people wanted any of them to leave the school. The vote for each of the three to stay was almost unanimous. They were suspended for a short time and not allowed to return until each of them had come in, with their parents, for a discussion with a small group consisting of two pupils and one teacher.

That was not the end of the story. Their behaviour improved a little, then deteriorated again. In the end one of them left to go abroad, one was taken away as a result of a parental decision, and the third stayed on and eventually found life very much easier.

The Lessons Learnt

What I learnt from all this was a great deal that I ought to have known already. When I was dealing with Peter I had assumed from the first that the meeting would not be able to cope with his behaviour, and that I would be a wiser and gentler authority. The meeting was never given a chance to deal with him directly. Now I know that that was a mistake. The meeting might well have come to the same decision as I did, but even so there would have been two gains. Firstly the children would have learnt from the discussion; they would have seen that their decisions were respected and that therefore it was essential to think responsibly. Secondly Peter would have seen that his offence was not against adult authority or a particular adult individual, but against the community as a whole. He would also have seen at first hand that the other children were really concerned for him. Forty heads are better than one, so it is likely that the meeting would have found a better solution than mine.

My other fear in Peter's case had been that no matter how dangerous his behaviour, the other children would never have asked him to leave. That fear was also proved ungrounded a couple of years later, when the school expelled someone for getting stoned with friends from the town during a morning break, and returning to school in that state. I also voted for this expulsion, because the offence happened just after a particularly strong resolution in a school meeting that the use of drugs was totally forbidden. Nevertheless I was afterwards uncertain as to whether the school had taken the right decision; this was someone who had only been in the school for a few weeks, who had had a very bad time at his previous school and who was also in some trouble outside school. In fact everything seems to have turned out well; the victim of expulsion returned later to visit the school without bearing any grudge, and, having passed the school-leaving age without further hassle, apparently making a success of life.

Before we started Sands I think I already knew that if you want children to take a share in the government of their schools then you have to give them real power. One of the things that went wrong at Dartington was a result of taking power away from the student body. It created a vicious circle. The children's deliberations had no effect, so there was no point in their deliberating seriously; their deliberations were not serious, so they could not expect them to be allowed to have any effect. If you reverse this circle you arrive at a much more useful situation. If your deliberations have effect, then you deliberate seriously; if you deliberate seriously, then your deliberations should be allowed to take effect.

Where I would have been cautious was in deciding in what areas such a virtuous circle would function effectively. As I have shown in the story of Peter, there was a time when I put clear limits to the amount of responsibility that I thought should be shared.

It now seems clear to me that there are no limits. When they need it, children ask for and accept the knowledge that comes from adults' experience. Adults who feel they have relevant experience that is being ignored can put forward their views for discussion. But what is important is that everyone's opinion should be given weight and taken seriously, and that in the end all big decisions should be a joint responsibility. The educational value of such discussions is beyond question enormous, but what is less often accepted, though on reflection it seems just as obvious, is that decisions made as a result of such discussion are bound to be better than decisions made without it.

The other theory that I would have propounded, optimistically but uncertainly, before Sands started, is that given the right power in the right school environment children would be just, generous, supportive and wise. In the five years that I worked at Sands I was often deeply moved by the demonstration of the truth of this.

CHAPTER SEVEN

THE FIRST CHILDREN'S HEARING

Inviting Children to Participate

In May 1990 the World Commission on Environment and Development held a regional follow-up conference in Bergen, in Norway. The conference was called "Our Common Future", and all the industrial world was represented. It was chaired by Gro Harlem Brundtland, leader of the Norwegian Labour Party, soon to become Prime Minister. The Norwegian Campaign for Environment and Development had the idea of inviting children to participate in the conference. The task of organising this participation fell to Kristin Eskeland. This is her account of the reasons behind the decision to involve children:-

Children are worried about the future. They know a lot about all the problems in the world and there is no way of escaping all the negative information about the state of the world.

Children are angry, they blame the grown up world for the problems, and rightly so. If we keep giving them all this depressing information, without giving them a realistic feeling that they themselves can do something about it, our children will at best grow up as a really aggressive group, who might use any means to produce a change. Or much worse they will turn into a frustrated, lethargic gang of people with no direction, no hope.

Therefore it is important to help them into situations where they can say what is on their minds, and say it to the people in charge.

Kristin got in touch with the most active children's organisations in Norway, and they appointed a steering committee and an editing group. They were determined to create an opportunity for children to speak for themselves, and were aware of the dangers of TV commercial cuteness and smooth adult manipulation. They did not want child actors reading texts written for them.

The first thing to do was to find out what issues children were worried about. They contacted all the schoolchildren in Norway aged between 7 and 16, and invited them to send in postcards to the Campaign for Environment and Development, with questions, drawings, poems, demands, statements; they were to put down whatever they wanted to say to the leaders of the world. About 6000 children responded.

Preparations

In the '70s young people's main anxiety had been the risk of nuclear war. By the '80s the focus had changed, and concerns ranged from Third World poverty to pollution at home. The editing group sorted all the children's cards under nine headings and picked out the most representative statements. Thirty-five of these statements were then chosen as "The Children's Environmental Appeal to World Leaders." The original wording was retained. The character of the appeal can be illustrated by a few quotations under some of the nine headings.

"General statements" was the first category. "Why can't we live like you did when you were small? Play in clean forests, fish in every lake, drink clean water straight from the stream?" "Life is more important than money."

Quotations about the Third World include "Wipe out the poor countries' foreign debts," and "The most important thing is equality between rich and poor countries."

Under various headings there are ideas that affect the children and their families directly. "We want better, cheaper public transport. Leave the car at home." "We must get better at re-using things." "Spend more money on cycle paths and footpaths."

The messages are simple and clear, and seem as relevant in 2006 as they were in 1990.

The completed document was translated into English, French and Russian, and the translations were printed and handed out to all the ministers who represented the various countries at the conference.

This was not the only way the message was delivered. Kristin proposed that they should also organise a public meeting between children and political leaders. The idea was accepted, and what developed became known as the Children's Hearing. It was a national rather than an international event, but it also took place during the "Our Common Future" conference. Ten children from different parts of the country aged between 12 and 15 were invited to speak, publicly, to six of Norway's most important people.

The selection of the ten children was a delicate business. Five came through the different children's organisations, and five through the schools. There are two peoples in Norway, Samis as well as Norwegians, so there were two Samis chosen. The idea was to present the viewpoint of ordinary children, so it was important not to select the elite who were able to act like little adults. Nevertheless participants needed to be genuinely concerned about questions of environment and development, and reasonably well-informed. Ideally there were to be representatives of rich and poor, town and country. The final team was Erik Almhjell, Trude Solheim, Karianne Frønsdal, Tone Bjørø Birkeland, Jon Cato Tevik, Mai-Bente Paulsen, Ida Oftebro, Nancy Porsanger, John-Aslak Kappfjell and Øyvind Nygård, six girls and four boys.

The group were shown the list of the statements raised on the postcards that had been sent in, and they each chose topics in which they themselves were particularly interested. The final list of issues was:-

Public transport and the building of motorways.

Water pollution from industry, agriculture and private homes.

Recycling and waste treatment.

The ozone layer and the pricing of environmentally sound and unsound products.

The environmental problems in Eastern Europe. What will Norway do?

Reduction of military expenditure, more to save the environment.

Environmental protection of the North Calotte: no to nuclear testing at Novaja Semlja.

North/South – the debt crisis.

Rain forests. What can Norway do to help the Indians?

A concert hall with seats for 1400 people was booked for the hearing. Trond-Viggo Torgersen, the Norwegian ombudsman for children, was asked to take the chair, to make sure that the children would be neither patronised, cowed nor out-talked by the politicians. Two experts on the environment from Bergen University were invited to sit on the platform to act as umpires when there was doubt over a matter of fact.

The power elite of Norway was asked to come to respond to the children. Gro Harlem Brundtland herself was invited. So were Arne Skauge, the Minister of Finance, Erik Solheim, another of the opposition leaders, Egil Myklebust, the head of the Association of Industrial Leaders and Bengt Martin Olsen, the Mayor of Bergen. They all came. The chairman of the Norwegian Trades Unions was invited, and sent his deputy, Esther Kostøl. The only person who turned down the invitation altogether was the head of the Norwegian Broadcasting Corporation.

The ten children who were to take part arrived the day before the hearing. Kristin had written to them, but she had never met them. They had a brief meeting in the concert hall to go over the programme and check that the microphones and lights were in order (they were not). Everything seemed rushed.

Each local school had been invited to send ten children, and invitations had also been sent to the press, some teachers and other interested adults. The occasion was also open to the general public. No one knew how many people would come.

The First Children's Hearing

In the event the 1400-seat hall was packed and the lights and microphones were fixed. On the platform were two long tables. At one sat the ten children, and at the other the adults. In front of each person, child or adult, was a placard bearing their first name in large letters, and their surname in smaller letters underneath. In his introduction the ombudsman asked the audience to make sure that their own ideas were expressed, to boo when they didn't understand or didn't agree, and to clap when they were pleased. There was entertainment as well as discussion, and the day started with the audience being invited to join in with some singing. This was followed by the first part of the hearing proper, and then there was a dance by some children from the Soviet School in Oslo before another round of questioning. So the hearing went on. With an interval, it lasted over three hours, and the audience was involved and enthusiastic throughout.

The adults tried to take the children seriously and to give them honest answers. This meant that there were very few promises of action. Mai-Bente Paulsen, who was twelve, suggested that the Minister for the Environment was not doing a satisfactory job, and should stand down. Arne Skauge, the Minister of Finance, was not ready to give a straight answer; we all do our best, he said, you cannot expect miracles, the Minister is doing everything possible. He was the only person on the platform who could be accused of being patronising.

The first part of the hearing dealt with local issues, and the questions were directed at the Mayor of Bergen. There had been a decision made to build a bridge out to the island of Askoy, just off the coast at Bergen. For environmental reasons many people who lived on the island did not want the bridge built, and Jon Cato Tevik asked the Mayor why the decision had been made against their wishes. The Mayor claimed that a majority had supported the bridge project. He was less able to cope with criticism of the decision to build an enormous underground car park under the festival park, a decision which was opposed by two-thirds of the citizens of the town. When he said that putting the cars underground would leave more open green spaces where the old car parks had been, and asked whether that wasn't a good idea, there were cries of "No" from the hall, and he changed his approach, saying that the decision was not yet finalised. Marianne Frønsdal, who had asked the original question, followed up with another about the pollution from car exhausts. To this he had no answer.

Mai-Bente Paulsen asked a question about the proposed environmental tax on the use of polluting chemicals, and received a vague reply about the need for people to trust one another. Trond-Viggo Torgersen intervened to make sure that the essence of the question was answered, asking whether the money raised by the environmental tax would in fact be earmarked for environmental protection. Arne Skauge replied that he could not promise this, and Mai-Bente asked, "What will you do with all that money when you have no world?" Again she received no clear reply, just the concession that no one could have a clear conscience and the news that he felt optimistic because there was soon to be a conference of finance ministers in Paris at which environmental issues would be discussed. "These are fine words," said Mai-Bente, "but you should support them with more courage."

The Sami girl, Nancy Porsanger, who lived in the north, asked about the nuclear testing just over the border in Russia. Gro Harlem Brundtland told her that the Norwegian government was talking with the Russians and trying to persuade them to stop, but that it was not a Norwegian decision and they could not do anything more than talk. John-Aslak Kappfjell, the other Sami, told the hearing that since Chernobyl it had not been safe to eat reindeer meat, and that this was causing real hardship to the Samis. He asked what extra precautions had been taken, and was simply told that not enough had been done. Tone Bjørø Birkeland rounded off this section of the discussion by saying that the only solution was to close down the atomic power-stations. The adults made no further comment.

Some Effects Of The Hearing

Over and over again the children raised issues in simple terms, and the adults had to try to respond clearly and convincingly, without resorting to criticism of their political opponents (the standby of all British politicians), over-technical language or barrages of abstract exhortation. The clarity of the discussion was exceptional.

The theme of the hearing was the environment and development, and the children showed much the same concerns as any well-informed adult, yet this was not like an ordinary political question-and-answer session. The children showed a sincerity, a concern and a lack of anxiety about image that the adults felt obliged to try to emulate. The occasion was an important success in two different ways:

1. As planned, the children were given the opportunity to meet important political figures and present the problems that worried them. This gave them some real influence on future decisions – not very much, but before they had had none. They were no longer passengers on a bus with a driver who refused to acknowledge their existence. Their special knowledge, their worries and their responsibility were at last being recognised.

2. The adults, who had come along to take part in an educational exercise for the benefit of the children, found that unexpected sincerity and clarity of thought were required of them. Instead of just feeling that they had presented their views once again, well or not so well, they found they were inspired by the children's approach and gained a great deal from the hearing themselves.

The first of these successes had been anticipated, but the second was a bonus, a surprise to many people, and redoubled the importance of the event.

When the hearing was over there was a march to the main hall where the international conference was being held. All the fourteen hundred participants marched across the city together, and when they arrived they presented the Children's Environmental Appeal to the world leaders who were assembled there. It was a powerful gesture and one that attracted the attention of the media, but it is unlikely that many of the politicians gave the appeal anything like the consideration it deserved, because they themselves had not had to respond to the children.

CHAPTER EIGHT

THE CHILDREN'S HEARING IN RIO

Preparation

After the Bergen hearing the Norwegian Campaign for Environment and Development joined up with the Environmental Defence Foundation (FUNAM) from Argentina to launch an international Voice of the Children campaign. The first objective was to encourage the organisation of Children's Hearings all over the world, and the second was to set up a Global Children's Hearing during the United Nations Conference for Environment and Development at Rio in 1992. Gro Harlem Brundtland wrote a letter of recommendation and they soon had the support of Maurice Strong, who was the secretary-general of the Rio conference, and James P. Grant, executive director of UNICEF.

Right from the beginning there was a determination that this occasion should not be used by politicians to get fresh publicity for their own opinions by having them expressed by children. The first letter inviting organisations to join ends: "We are specially concerned that the campaign must be on the children's own premises, that the adult organisers really listen to children, and make sure that the questions being raised are the children's own." In a later letter Kristin Eskeland wrote, "My greatest fear has been that adults will use this campaign in their own interest. It is vital to remember that the role of the organisers of Children's Hearings is to facilitate, to acquire the children's own views without adult coaxing or pressure. No matter how well organised a Children's Hearing may seem, it is a failure if it may be said that it was a show staged to please the adults, or that the children were only saying what their grown-up leaders wanted them to say."

It was suggested that each country should set up a National Committee which would co-ordinate local action, collect children's opinions for a National Children's Appeal and organise a National Hearing.

In the campaign's Guide for Local Action it was again stressed that it was the children's opinions that were wanted, not anyone else's. The organisers were asked to invite any children, preferably between the ages of 12 and 16, to take part if they were genuinely interested in the campaign. One of the activities suggested was brainstorming: a group of ten to fifteen children would be invited to say whatever came into their minds on the subject of environment and development. The instructions to the organisers were "Write down whatever is said, *don't comment, no matter what they say,* even if you don't like it. Just write it down." Later there is a more general recommendation: "Make sure the children feel that they are being supported by people who take them seriously."

There was also concern expressed about the possibility of inadequate response from the politicians at the hearings. "Don't let the grown ups get away with patronising answers or promises they don't intend to keep." Hearings should be chaired by someone whose task is "to help the children follow up their arguments to make sure the grown-ups don't get away with evasions and half truths."

By February 1992 thirty countries had joined the campaign. The committee selected twenty of these countries to be invited to send representatives to the Global Hearing at Rio. The countries were chosen in order to be sure of some balance between different parts of the world, and each of them was asked to find a child who had been active in the campaign, and to look beyond the middle class, so that there should be children who did not go to school as well as school-children, children from poor families as well as wealthy ones.

As well as speaking at the hearing, the delegation was to present the *Children's Appeal to World Leaders*, the text of which may be found in Appendix Three of this book.

Arriving in Rio

The conference involved the leaders of the world, including US President George Bush senior. Its full name was the United Nations Conference for Environment and Development, but it was generally known as the Earth Summit.

It was held in Rio Centro, an hour away from the centre of the town. A new road was built from Rio, avoiding the slums so that the delegates would get a good impression. Many of the street children and others living on the street were moved out of the city for the duration of the summit. Soldiers with machine-guns stood at intervals along all the main streets and beaches.

Right in the town itself was the Global Forum, a combined conference and exhibition that was housed in tents and booths in a park overlooking the beach. This alternative venue was for non-governmental organisations of all kinds, for example charities, pressure groups and aid agencies. One of the meetings in the main marquee at the Global Forum was to be the Global Children's Hearing.

The children really did come from all over the world. There were fourteen girls and seven boys. This is a list of the countries they represented, their names and their ages. Their surnames were not published, because some came from countries where the government actively disapproved of their participation.

Argentina	Hector	8
Australia	May	12
Brazil	Andrea	12
Canada	Yuri	14
Chile	Marcela	12
Colombia	Ana	11

	Carmen	17
France	Julien	14
Germany	Björn	14
	Bettina	16
Guatemala	Sayda	11
Latvia	Dite	12
Malta	Jamie	12
New Zealand	Rema	14
Nigeria	Anietie Phillip	14
Norway	Mai-Bente	14
Philippines	Sylvia Trina	14
Rwanda	Marthe-Olive	12
Uganda	Andrew	9
Ukraine	Alina	11
USA	John	14

They began to arrive, a few at a time, on May 28th, just over a fortnight before the hearing, each accompanied by a parent or guardian. They stayed in the Collegio Assunçao, a convent on the top of one of the mountains in the middle of Rio, overlooking Sugarloaf Mountain, the sea and the city in one direction and in the other overlooked by the gigantic statue of Christ crucified that dominates the city from the next mountain. Here they were welcomed by the representatives of Voice of the Children, Kristin Eskeland, Heather Saddler and Sarah McCrum. (Sarah and Kristin are the sources of my information.)

How they Spent their Time
Language was much less of a divisive factor than might have been expected. What they needed from each other was utterly international; it was love and friendship. The main languages were English, French and Spanish, but the girls from Latvia and the Ukraine could speak none of them; they

depended on their interpreters, and when they were not there, on body language and facial expressions. In the group as a whole there was a great deal of hand-holding, hugging and laughter, and when the time came to leave there were many tears. The children showed great independence, and organised their own free time without waiting for guidance from their guardians or the staff. Late in the evening there was a regular unofficial meeting on the roof, where talk went on into the early hours.

Each day events were arranged. The whole group went to the beach and did a little sight-seeing. They spent a day with children from a smart private school, and they met two different groups of street children. They could not fail to see the slums, the favelas, which reached up the hill where they were staying, and some visited them. Brazilian children from both ends of the social spectrum joined the group for some of their outings.

Since many of them had never been abroad before at all, these were powerful experiences. The first-hand encounter with poverty was a major shock for several of them; Jamie, the Maltese boy, was appalled to find that the street children, who were ordinary and companionable like himself, had literally nowhere to live, and commented on this to Sarah; Mai-Bente, the Norwegian representative, dropped her proposed topic of nuclear power in order to speak about poverty at the hearing.

Part of the children's time was of course spent preparing specifically for the hearing. They were all aware of having been chosen to represent their countries, and had come with clear ideas about what they wanted to say, or perhaps in some cases, in spite of the careful advice against it, what they were expected to say. Alina from the Ukraine was herself a Chernobyl child; Marthe-Olive from Rwanda had seen her brother and sister shot and injured in war; Andrew, from Uganda, was prepared with information about the dumping of expired medicines.

Voice of the Children tried to make sure that what they said at the hearing was indeed what they themselves felt, and not what they had been taught to recite. The adults emphasised that they were there for the children, and not the other way round. The children met in groups for discussion, generally without adult intervention; sometimes adults were excluded altogether, sometimes there were joint discussions and sometimes the adults were allowed to attend but not to contribute – some found this difficult. There was a role-playing session for the children, in which groups divided up into petitioners and politicians; those playing politicians lied unscrupulously and denied all responsibility for anything that had gone wrong.

The children were urged to avoid asking questions when they spoke, because when you ask questions you give the politicians a chance to say whatever they want. They were encouraged to speak as much as possible from personal experience, and not to launch into generalities; whenever children said anything that seemed to come particularly directly from the heart, they were praised. There was discussion as to how the hearing itself should be organised, what order they should speak in, how they should sit on the platform but in the event the stage was much smaller than expected, all the chairs had been arranged in two rows and instead of six microphones there were only two. The children coped without anxiety. On the day before the hearing they practised their speeches in pairs, each listening to the other and trying to make helpful comments. There was no adult guidance as to subject matter.

Official Attitudes

By the day of the hearing they had already had a good deal of experience of public speaking and some clear demonstrations of public support and official neglect. The opening of the Global Forum was a children's occasion, and the grounds were full of children, yet not one of the speakers addressed either the children or anything relating to children. Five children were invited to take part, one of whom was Marthe Olive, from Voice of the Children. All they had to do was read short passages from a book of statements from other children that had been collected from around the world by a group called Gaia. Marthe-Olive chose the statement she wanted to read and reworded it a little.

Maurice Strong, who set up the Earth Summit, had originally supported the idea that children should be involved. In the event not one was asked to participate. Kristin Eskeland had to negotiate for some children to take part in the opening ceremony, and in the end a group of five was invited. The children were excited about this until they discovered that all they were to do was to raise a flag, and that the flag-raising was to be done before the adult participants in the conference were due to arrive. The night before the opening they sat up late making banners – "We are the future", "We want to participate" – and they all set off for Rio Centro. When they arrived they were too late for the flag-raising; the five prospective flag-raisers were admitted, and spent an hour talking to the press inside. The others sat in front of the registration desk, raised their banners, sang songs and spoke to the press outside. The press was extremely enthusiastic.

The Australian Minister for the Environment visited them and though she started by making a speech herself she also had time to listen. During her visit she offered a striking example of political blindness about an issue on which the children she was addressing were better informed than she was. She was asked why the street children were not at the conference, and she said she did not believe there were any. Andrea, the Brazilian representative, knew that many of the street children had been moved out, and had seen photographs of dead children on television, children who had been killed by the police. This is how she described what happened next:

> So I said to see the poverty in Rio she couldn't have looked in front of the convent. She started to laugh, and I said she was saying what all government people say ... doing what they all do trying to take us all in. She started out thinking everyone would believe what she was saying, taking us in, setting us up so when the Congress came, people would speak well of Brazil, and when the other, our president, went there he'll speak well of Australia, saying Australia's perfect and all that ... so she was protecting Brazil ... saying there was no poverty or anything.

The French environment minister gave them a carefully timed five minutes in a room where there was a luxurious buffet set out, and at the end of the five minutes gave them pizzas in grey paper bags. They left as quickly as they could.

Maurice Strong himself promised half an hour to meet several groups of children in front of the press, and left after ten minutes, when presumably he felt they had got enough photographs. Once again, the children were left alone with the reporters and audience and made a powerful impression.

The final and most damaging effect of official neglect was a change in dates. The Children's Hearing at the Global Forum had been deliberately arranged for the day before Bush's address to the Earth Summit. At the last minute, Bush's appearance was advanced by a day. This meant that all the world leaders and most of the press had to be at Rio Centro, an hour's drive away from the hearing.

The Hearing Itself

The four politicians on the platform at the Children's Hearing were Luiza Erundina, the mayor of Sao Paulo, from Brazil, Michael Bohnet, a director of development aid from Germany, Erik Solheim, a Socialistic Left member of the Norwegian parliament and Senator Al Gore from the United States, who did not then know that he would soon be vice-president. The chair was taken by Kate Lyra, an American who had lived in Brazil for many years, and was in charge of the children's activities at the Global Forum.

The hearing started with a performance by a group of street children who sang and acted a play which included a parody of the press's treatment of them, in which they all pulled their jerseys up over their faces, as they always do, to avoid being identified in photographs. The Voice of the Children speakers and the adult panel then introduced themselves.

The children were divided into five groups, dealing with different topics. The topics were poverty, education, war and violence, pollution and the environment. Direct questions were to be answered by the panel immediately, but otherwise they were to wait till a group had finished its presentation before making comments. Virtually every important environmental issue was accounted for – the division of wealth between north and south, the protection of the rain forest, respect for indigenous peoples, nuclear power, water pollution, global warming, war and the manufacture of armaments, toxic waste, the protection of wildlife and so on. What was said was not new, but it was given a new clarity and urgency by the young speakers. I have heard a recording and it is extremely moving. I am told that many of the audience were in tears.

The children stated facts simply:

My country is now experiencing an extreme poverty. We all know that because of poverty a lot of people die. Mostly our children. – *Sylvia, Philippines*

The drugs are expired and are killing more and more children. ... Do
you want this killing from expired medicines to happen? – *Andrew, Uganda*

The world is divided in two, a rich world and a poor world. And it is
not fair. Unfortunately, the poor world is larger. The rich have an
unacceptable lifestyle, the excessive consumption of limited
resources. – *Julien, France*

My name is Alina, I am 11 and a member of the organisation Green
Help. I live in Ukraine, 100 kilometres out of Chernobyl. That is why
I want to raise the question about atomic power which is most painful
for us. – *Alina, Ukraine*

What concerns me most on my reservation is the violence against the
indigenous people. More and more of them are being killed. For me it
is horrible when they kill five, four, three or twenty-five at a time.
– *Ana, Colombia*

When you listen to the recording it is impressive to hear the politicians
making serious answers to the children's questions, but you realise that they
had to when you hear how the questions were followed up, courteously but
insistently, if the answers were not satisfactory. Sometimes it was straightforward. Jamie from Malta asked, "Would you promise to do everything
you can to reinforce the laws regarding pollution and take serious actions?"
and Al Gore said, "I'd be glad to make that promise," and Erik Solheim
said, "Definitely, yes." Over the question about expired medicines Al Gore
confessed ignorance, and said, "I would personally like to look into this
and see what can be done about it." When Dite from Latvia asked for a
global declaration of environmental education the idea was welcomed.
On the other hand Björn, from Germany, was not satisfied.

Often the governments spend more money on destruction and building
weapons than on protection of nature. So could the right-thinking
man, or woman, think it is good to spend more money on destruction
and death of other people than on protection of nature? So my
question to every one of these politicians is: How much money does

your government spend on the military and how much on protection of nature? Do you think it is good so? What will you do against this?

The politicians spoke at some length, agreeing with his general point of view, but to the delight of the audience, Björn persisted.

I asked you how much money. I always get the answer "a lot of money" or "not so much money". Can you give us numbers, so that we can hear the difference.

In much shorter replies, the politicians said that in Norway they spent three times as much on defence as on development aid, and ten times as much as on the environment. In Germany the corresponding ratios are ten to one and five to one. Al Gore gave only one ratio, approximately one hundred to one. In Brazil, according to Luiza Erundina, expenditure on arms had stopped with the end of the military dictatorship.

Alina from the Ukraine asked why nothing had been done at the conference in Rio Centro to stop military and civil nuclear programmes. The question was ignored until Kate Lyra, the chairperson, pointed out towards the end of the hearing that it had not been answered. When Erik Solheim said it was because some powers didn't want the issue raised, but that he thought that if money was spent on research into sustainable energy great improvements would result, Alina said, "I want to know when that is supposed to be done." Al Gore said it must be done now. Alina asked, "What do you do with nuclear waste?" and the politicians were all silent.

This direct simplicity and clarity were part of what made the occasion so impressive, but some of the speakers also spoke with a passion that was impossible to ignore. Quotations without the desperate insistence of the young voices are bound to lose something, but perhaps you can imagine words like these spoken by serious, sincere children who know that what they are saying matters perhaps more than anything they have ever said before.

Still two thirds of the world's population need shelter, food, education and medical care. We have lost sight of mankind and fought wars. We practise discrimination on the basis of our skin colour, we need to know that we are all equal, and that we are treated the same. Before we can change the way we live, before we have saved the rainforest and the whales, we need to change ourselves. Humanity with all its different races is one. We and all other living things are nourished and sustained by the same earth. This is our salvation, this is our responsibility. How can we turn our back on Mother Earth? – *Rema, New Zealand*

That's what it's all about, not just any old future but the future of the planet earth and our future. I'd say nothing special will come of ECO 92 but it might be a start. You can't look at things the way governments talk, but how Brazilian people suffer. Ecology isn't just green, it's red, too: the red of the blood of the suffering people of Brazil. – *Andrea, Brazil*

We can only stop poverty if the politicians stop thinking about money, power, and all those big houses. I think politicians should start opening their eyes. Hear the children crying. I think they should put love in their hearts, not fire, not money, not greediness and not corruption. – *Sylvia, Philippines*

Children are tired of seeing so much violence. We don't want any more war. We want peace, fraternity and harmony among all human beings. Please. Look at what you're doing to the world we live in. You're making the world such a bad place and children so sad. It's terrible. God left us such a beautiful world, and was it only for us to destroy it from end to end? No. That's not right. For God's sake, let's realise what we are doing. Please! – *Sayda, Guatemala*

I did not speak any Spanish when I heard this recording, but I quickly learnt the words for please: Por favor. Sayda cried it out, twice, and it is hard to forget.

A Final Quotation

The last quotation I want to make is from Marthe-Olive, aged 12, from Rwanda. She spoke in French, so what follows is a translation. She spoke calmly and clearly, in a matter-of-fact way, without apparent emotion.

> My name is Marthe-Olive. I come from Rwanda. I want to talk about the problems that I have in Rwanda. For years the children of Rwanda have been unhappy because of the war. They have seen children like themselves die, little ones and big ones, men and women. Lots of families are scattered. They have left their possessions to get away from the guns and the bombs. Now they have no shelter, no food, no clothes. They have nothing. Some children have become orphans and no one takes care of them. Others, their schools have been destroyed and they do not know where to go. We do not want to live in this war, in this misery. Wars kill innocent people, they spread disorder and hatred. They slow down development. Children do not like war. Those in Rwanda want the war to end very soon so that people can live in peace. Thank you.

This speech was translated from French into Portuguese by a professional translator. He began in the expressionless way interpreters speak, occasionally hesitating over a choice of word, sounding like a student doing a translation exercise, and then suddenly he was overcome by the meaning of what he was saying, and he was unable to go on. When the audience appreciated his emotion they applauded, and he went on a little before having to stop again, and then finished the last couple of sentences with an incoherent rush ending in tears.

Al Gore later commented on this incident, and said he had been much moved. He attributed the interpreter's emotion to fully realising the pain and the suffering in her homeland that this young girl was describing.

Marthe-Olive did not describe her own suffering in particular, and she did not ask for sympathy. She simply reported the suffering of the children of Rwanda. What disturbs us so deeply as adults when we hear her message is that all of a sudden we are made to understand what the word war actually means. There is no euphemism, there is no political vindication, there is simply a straightforward statement of the facts. The normal adult detachment becomes impossible, and once we have lost our detachment then the sentence, "Children do not like war," becomes an indictment of our former attitude. We are suddenly restored to a simpler ethical system where the ultimate wrong is to cause suffering, and all political excuses become unacceptable. "[Children] in Rwanda want the war to end very soon so that people can live in peace."

An atmosphere had been established at the Hearing in which children's voices were heard and their opinions were listened to seriously. What I think happened during the translation of Marthe-Olive's words was that the interpreter found himself saying things that are obvious to anybody, but that we usually take great care to avoid noticing. Adults are trained to accept political explanations, to foresee complications, to put power before people, but when they actually listen with respect to someone who does none of these things, they see at once how wrong they have been. Normally we are able to ignore such voices, but the Rio hearing had created a situation in which that was impossible. The interpreter found himself speaking words that echoed in his own heart, words that he recognised as containing an important truth, a truth that if it were more widely understood might even bring the war to an end. What he was weeping at was, I think, the sudden recognition of an ideal, and the realisation that it had for so long been scorned as an irrelevance.

We don't like children to watch the horrors on the news because, we say, it affects them too strongly. We feel we can take it, but what this actually means is that we are able to ignore it. It is only as adults that we are able to turn our backs on huge differences in wealth, starvation in the third world, the risk of nuclear war, the prospect of climate change. When we say that we don't want children to have to face such prospects we are actually protecting ourselves from the perfectly rational distress and fear that younger people have not yet learned to suppress.

An eleven-year-old girl at Caol Primary School in Scotland, Jodie Fraser, was ill at home on 9.11 when the twin towers in New York were attacked. She watched it on television, and when she got back to school she went up to the school's famous art room, Room 13, and created a work of art. She took a big canvas and scattered over it 3000 burnt matchsticks, one for each person who had died, and then sprayed it with grey paint for smoke. It is an extremely impressive work, and has been exhibited in many different galleries in the UK, including Tate Modern, the main modern art museum in London. Jodie Fraser, eleven years old at the time, said, "I wanted to do a painting that would make people cry."

Most of us adults do not cry about current events, however awful they are.

I wrote in Chapter Five of the walls which adults build around their own moral awareness, so that they are not interrupted by awkward demands from their consciences. It seems that children are capable of pulling those walls down. Children are the guardians of the conscience of mankind.

CHAPTER NINE

THE DISCOVERY

At the beginning of this book I said that I had never before dared to express "this idea", with the implication that "this idea" was merely that adults do not have a monopoly on wisdom, and children's opinions ought to be taken seriously. That is a moderate view.

This is the discovery I had actually made, and that I was too timid to put into words in Chapter One.

Adults do not pass moral values on to their children. In moral matters, children are better judges than grown-ups. The best we can do as adults is to relearn from our children the values that we ourselves once held.

CHAPTER TEN

OBJECTIONS

In spite of being certain about my discovery, I worry about the negative evidence. This chapter and the following one are more for my own reassurance than to further the argument. They present a series of objections to what I have just written, followed by my responses. They do not further the argument because this is not a fair way of arguing; I can express the objections as foolishly as I like, and I always give myself the last word. Nevertheless, by articulating some of the most obvious criticisms, followed at least by denials if not by total refutations, I shall show that I have not simply overlooked them.

My first fear is that I may be accused of sentimentality; I have even quoted a hackneyed passage from Wordsworth.

Objection One

Wordsworth was a nineteenth-century poet, and what's worse, a romantic poet. That whole *Intimations of Immortality* bit is a load of sentimental guff, full of joyous birds and bounding lambs, rainbows, happy shepherd boys and jollity. Anyone who takes all that seriously is bound to be a bit soft. It's all wishful thinking, and the idea that children are the conscience of mankind is unrealistic to the point of idiocy.

Response

Of course I know that there is a sentimental view of children as sweet and pretty, and therefore angelic. Wordsworth was not writing sentimentally in *Intimations of Immortality*, in spite of the rainbow and the bounding lambs. He was not looking at other children, he was remembering his own childhood, and recalling a vividness of perception that he had lost. This was not only a matter of what he saw and heard, it also included "those obstinate questionings of sense and outward things", high instincts that he had all but forgotten. It is with moral perceptions in particular that I have been concerned, but I have not made any suggestion that children are sweet, pretty and angelic, and nor did Wordsworth.

There is even scientific support for the Wordsworthian view. I quote from *How Babies Think*:

> We hope our view of babies is not too romantic, but it is certainly Romantic. We think "Intimations of Immortality" [Wordsworth] and "Auguries of Innocence" [Blake] may, in fact, describe just what it is like to be a child. That's the way the world looked when your brain had 15,000 synapses per neuron and burned up twice as much glucose. And that is still, at least sometimes, what it's like to be human, even if it takes the form only of intimations and auguries.

Objection Two

Children are horrible little brats. Babies scream when they don't get what they want, toddlers bite and scratch and pull the cat's tail and snatch and spill and break, young children steal and fight and lie and cheat, older children watch TV all day, never put anything away, disobey, swear and refuse to do the washing up or go to bed at the right time, young adolescents smoke and miss school and bully younger kids and demand expensive presents and then after that they get on to all-night raves and alcohol and drugs and sex and life for their parents is a nightmare until they finally grow up and find partners and settle down to rear families of their own.

Response

It is true that children sometimes do horrible brattish things, but so do adults. It is also true that they are sometimes thoughtful, generous and wise. In between times their behaviour is presumably morally neutral. Adults are sometimes domineering and self-centred and sometimes affectionate and understanding. It is not reasonable to condemn an entire age-group because of occasional lapses on the part of some of its members.

Objection Three
What about bullying?

Response

In *The Hothouse Society*, Royston Lambert's research into boarding schools, he found that the worst bullying happened in schools where the staff themselves used violence as a method of discipline.

Children themselves do not take bullying lightly. I have been shown a letter written by a teacher to her class of thirteen-year-olds after a long discussion about it. Here are some extracts.

The following week we talked about why people bully. Your responses were amazing. You said that people bully because:

they have problems at home which they can't deal with and so take it out on people at school; they feel insecure and this is their only

way of getting an image; they are being humiliated by someone
bigger and stronger and so want to humiliate someone less strong
in order to maintain 'face'; they want to look 'big' in front of their
friends; they want revenge; they find someone irritating; they're
cowards; they're jealous; they feel inadequate in some way; it makes
them look hard; if you feel inadequate it's comforting to know
that you can make others feel inadequate; they are bossy and like
to have their own say; they are unhappy for some reason and get
into bad moods. You also said that school is like the rest of
society. There are bullies 'out there'; the world is a competitive
place where most people are prepared to put others down in order
to better themselves.

This list of possibilities is enough to remind us that bullying is not a
simple matter of a nasty proclivity towards making others suffer, and
shows a generous thoughtfulness on the part of the victims. Later in the
letter the teacher printed two general conclusions in thick black type:

**People who are not treated with respect will not behave respectfully.
According to you then, we create bullies. It is a way for some to take
the respect that is denied them by parents or teachers or peers.**

According to me too.

Objection Four

It's all very well to say that children often take the high moral ground in
discussion – that just shows what dreadful little hypocrites they are. Fourteen-year-olds who say they are concerned about the environment aren't
sufficiently concerned to stop throwing their coke cans into the gutters.
Children who fuss about ponies being exported to French butchers are
perfectly happy to eat cow when it arrives cooked on the table. Fifteen-
year-olds who smoke criticise twelve-year-olds for smoking, bullies moan
about bullying, truants are shocked by the amount of truancy, cannabis-
smokers disdain glue-sniffers. Children don't give all their pocket-money

to charities, so why do they expect anything better from adults? Anyone can take a high-minded attitude; what counts is not what you say but what you do.

Response

The complaint that children criticise society but then do nothing about it is hardly a complaint against the children themselves. They would do something if they could, but society has made sure that they are powerless. When children are shown a means of achieving change, they will often put in a great deal of energy; when they feel they have no power there is little point in trying. The objection that an adolescent who complains about nuclear dumping in the Irish Sea then throws a drink-can into the hedge seems to be more an example of an adult's deviousness than a description of the adolescent's hypocrisy: the difference in scale is so huge that the argument could only have been invented by a tidy-minded adult looking for a new reason for discouraging children from dropping litter.

Objection Five

Children don't help around the house. They may have high-flown moral ideas, but they don't apply them in practice. When you need something useful done, it's better to ask a grown-up. Children are naturally unhelpful, and have no perseverance. Suppose, by some extraordinary chance, you happen upon a child who appears to be ready to take on some necessary but boring job, such as scrubbing a floor or digging a vegetable patch. You'll be lucky if you get half an hour's work done.

Response

Small children are eager to be helpful, but because their help is often something of a hindrance, adults deliberately train them not to help. Helping is thought of as getting in the way. It is unreasonable to train someone not to do something, and later to complain because they don't do it.

When they reach their teens, children are often asked to undertake tasks that would otherwise be done by their parents; that is not so much helping as serving. When parents are ill or handicapped, children do everything that is necessary, including the nursing.

To accuse children of lack of perseverance is simply blindness. Children lack persistence in tasks that they do not like and that they have not chosen to do, which may well include scrubbing the floor and digging the vegetable patch. Adults who are faced with tasks that do not seem important to them, such as arranging and re-arranging the furniture in a doll's house, or picking up something a baby keeps throwing on the ground, or learning a computer game, will lose interest after only a few minutes, whereas children may carry on with it for hours. Hardly any adults had the persistence to learn to handle the Rubik cube. All those people who regret not having learnt a musical instrument when they were children lack the patience and persistence to sit down and practise now. How many of us have ever got beyond lesson four of a teach-yourself language course? It is not that children have less persistence than adults, it is that they are more often required to tackle tasks which of no interest to them for no reward – tasks, what is more, that they have been taught to see as the responsibility of adults.

Objection Six

What about crime? Most crime is committed by juveniles. What about housing estates which have become almost uninhabitable because of the persistent robbery and vandalism?

Response

Most crime may be committed by juveniles, but most juveniles do not commit crime.

Nevertheless, there are places where juvenile crime seems to be the norm. The Swiss psychiatrist Alice Miller has an authoritative explanation. She claims, in *Banished Knowledge*, that anti-social behaviour is created by grown-ups, and suggests that this process may start at birth.

So-called difficult, 'insufferable' children have been turned into such by adults. Not always by their own parents: obstetrical and postpartum practices in many hospitals are often the first to contribute in large measure to this process. Some parents are able to compensate for these traumas by means of loving care, because they take them seriously and do not deny their danger.

In an appendix to *The Drama of Being a Child*, she describes the process further:

1. All children are born to grow, to develop, to live, to love, and to articulate their needs and feelings for their self-protection.

2. For their development children need the respect and protection of adults who take them seriously, love them, and honestly help them to become oriented in the world.

3. When these vital needs are frustrated and children are instead abused for the sake of adults' needs by being exploited, beaten, punished, taken advantage of, manipulated, neglected, or deceived without the intervention of any witness, then their integrity will be lastingly impaired.

4. The normal reactions to such injury should be anger and pain; since children in this hurtful kind of environment, however, are forbidden to express their anger and since it would be unbearable to experience their pain all alone, they are compelled to suppress their feelings, repress all memory of the trauma, and idealize those guilty of the abuse. Later they will have no memory of what was done to them.

5. Disassociated from their original cause, their feelings of anger, helplessness, despair, longing, anxiety, and pain will find expression in destructive acts against others (criminal behaviour, mass murder) or against themselves (drug addiction, alcoholism, prostitution, psychic disorders, suicide.)

In the last paragraph Alice Miller is writing about adults; it is hardly surprising that children feeling the same anger, helplessness, despair, longing, anxiety and pain should respond with burglary, bullying and graffiti.

Objection Seven
What about the boys who killed Jamie Bulger?

Response

Two ten-year-old boys killed a toddler by throwing bricks at him and leaving him on a railway line. It was all over the national press for weeks. During the same period an adult male was in court for attacking his wife, using their baby, wrapped in a pillow-case, as a cosh. I have not met anyone else who even noticed the short item at the bottom of a newspaper column where I read about this. Adults behaving badly are not news.

The NSPCC reckons that in Britain a child is killed by its parents or carers every two days. Imagine how many children must be seriously injured. The wonder is not that two boys have killed a toddler, it is that other abused children have behaved with such restraint.

Objection Eight
What about Columbine High?

Response

Two teenagers came into their school armed with guns, shot and killed twelve of their fellow-pupils and one teacher, and then turned their guns upon themselves. It was horrifying.

If you can find me any healthy, happy children who do not think it was horrifying, then I will agree that you are right to be worried about the younger generation.

I don't think you will find them. What worries me is that there were once plenty of healthy, happy adult Germans who believed that it was right to exterminate the Jews and there are still plenty of healthy, happy adult Arabs who believe that it is right to stone an adulteress to death and plenty of healthy, happy adult Americans who believe that it was right to drop nuclear bombs on Hiroshima and Nagasaki.

Objection Nine

What about *The Lord of the Flies*? On the back cover of my edition *The Times* reviewer is quoted as saying 'Mr. Golding knows exactly what boys are like; he has a compelling imagination; and the vivid realism with which he describes the disintegration of their untried and precarious civilisation under the pressure of raw nature carries the reader to the bloody climax ... a most absorbing and instructive tale.'

Response

The Lord of the Flies is so often quoted as if it were proof of the universality of childish savagery that I have re-read it carefully. People even talk about the Lord-of-the-Flies syndrome, a supposed tendency among boys to revert to primitive nastiness when they are not under adult control, evidence for which is thought to be found in William Golding's novel. Perhaps, since a novel can't be evidence for anything except its author's opinions, it would be better to say that whatever evidence there may be lies in adult reaction to the novel, rather than in the novel itself.

The story concerns a group of boys who are left stranded on a fertile island in the tropics as the result of an attack on an aeroplane. At first, under the leadership of a boy called Ralph, they make some attempt to build shelters and keep a signal fire alight on top of the central hill, but soon they are led into savagery by another boy called Jack Merridew who begins by killing pigs and painting his face with coloured clay, and ends up creating a tribe of his own which he rules with violent discipline. Two boys are actually killed by the tribe, and soon Ralph is the only survivor who does not belong. The book ends with him fleeing from a fire which the others have lit to drive him out of the forest so that they can kill him too. He runs out onto the shore into the arms of a British naval officer who has seen the fire and come to investigate. It is an extremely exciting adventure story with a tremendous final chase, two forest fires, a dead parachutist, a thunderstorm and the slaughter of animals and children.

The Times critic says "Mr. Golding knows exactly what boys are like," and commends the book for its vivid realism. In fact the book offers no evidence at all that Mr. Golding knows what boys are like, and far from being realistic it is clearly a fantasy; it has such marked characteristics of fantasy that I cannot believe there was ever any intention to make it realistic.

At the beginning of the book there are a number of children on a deserted island. They have arrived there uninjured, having emerged, as far as I can make out, from a tube that was dropped from a damaged plane; the tube was then immediately dragged out to sea by a storm, and it plays no further part in the story. The children have been scattered about the island and gradually assemble. Except for a party from a choir school who all somehow managed to land together, none of them know each other, or even recognise each other from the aeroplane. No one has any baggage except for the members of the choir school, who have their cassocks as well as their school uniforms. No one has any difficulty in finding food or water. A few have died unlamented in the crash, but otherwise no one is seriously hurt. The palms provide shelter from the sun, the rocks have created a perfect swimming pool and wild pigs have made convenient paths through the forest where they can apparently be killed for food without danger.

When the boys first meet they do not discuss the accident or tell each other of their own adventures. They show no anxiety about their position and no concern for the rest of the passengers who must have been dragged out to sea in the tube. The number of boys on the island is never specified; only four are clearly characterised, though a few others are given names; for the most part they are divided into two groups – biguns, the eldest of whom are 12, and littluns, who are always described as "about six". No one seems to feel any responsibility for anyone else, though Piggy, the inhibited, unhealthy, socially inept intellectual who really knows what ought to be done, does share mild concern with Ralph when they notice that one of the littluns has disappeared at the time of the forest fire. The other three characterised boys are Ralph himself, the confident, good-looking, athletic leader with a vague awareness that action needs to be taken, Jack Merridew, the aggressive, arrogant head prefect of the choir school and Simon, a shy, solitary boy who has fits and a sense of the numinous. The story can be seen as the victory of Jack Merridew over the other three – the victory of violence over intellect, responsibility and religion. It is plainly a fable and not a realistic account.

At the end of the book Ralph weeps "for the end of innocence, the darkness of man's heart, and the fall through the air of a true, wise friend called Piggy." The story is intended to exemplify the darkness of man's heart, not the darkness of children's hearts. It is a pity that it is generally taken as an exemplification of the latter, and often not merely as an exemplification but as a kind of proof.

My quarrel is not with William Golding, but with the interpretation people like to put on his book. Unfortunately this means that I have to attack the view that he knew what boys were like. He must have known he was on unfamiliar ground, because he was extremely cautious about specifying their ages. Nevertheless he slipped up from time to time. Ralph, aged twelve, believes that his father will come and rescue them when he has leave from the Navy. Piggy, whose age is never given but who appears to be only slightly younger, takes this belief seriously. There are other instances of inappropriate naiveté elsewhere in the book. At one point Jack Merridew, also aged 12, says "I ought to be chief because I'm chapter chorister and head boy. I can sing C sharp." Ralph says, "The Queen has a big room full of maps and all the islands of the world are drawn there. So the Queen's got a picture of this island." It is a little embarrassing.

All the boys except Ralph, Piggy, Simon and sometimes the characterless twins, Sam and Eric, prefer swimming and lazing around to exploring or doing anything constructive. Few real children of this age like lazing around; they adapt their environment, they build shelters and furniture, they investigate, they invent, they fish, they organize games, they experiment with cooking, they make plans. William Golding was not writing Robinson Crusoe or Coral Island, he was writing a fable, and for his fable he needed an aimless group of idlers, so that is what he created. It is not, and nor can it have been intended to be, a realistic picture of a group of children.

There is a slight suggestion that it is the absence of adult authority that leads to the eventual abandonment of civilised values. Maurice, an uncharacterised bigun, accidentally kicks sand into the face of a littlun, and "Now, though there was no parent to let fall a heavy hand,

Maurice still felt the unease of wrongdoing." Roger, a little later, throwing stones to drop in the water all round a littlun, finds his arm "conditioned by a civilization that knew nothing of him. ... Here, invisible yet strong, was the taboo of the old life." From the first example one might imagine that William Golding appreciated that "the unease of wrongdoing" is a more powerful instrument than "a heavy hand", but from the second it seems clear that he thought the only reason for not throwing stones at a small child was "the taboo of the old life."

If it was really his intention to illustrate this idea, in the book as a whole he subconsciously betrayed a different awareness. Of his four fully characterised boys, three resist the call of savagery. It is only the uncharacterised mob that follows Jack Merridew. Jack himself is the source of all the drive towards violence and primitivism. And who is Jack Merridew? He is the chapter chorister and head boy. He can sing C sharp. The authority which stays with them from the world they have left behind them does not keep the boys from savagery; it leads them directly into it.

The Times critic was right about one thing. It is an instructive book. It is a pity that so many people have misunderstood the instruction.

A Brief Excursion Into Etymology

Philanthropy means a love of mankind, and philogyny means a love of woman-kind. A Francophile is someone who loves the French and a bibliophile is someone who loves books. A paedophile is someone who desires children sexually.

A misanthropist is someone who hates mankind, a misogynist is someone who hates womankind, and we have no word for someone who hates children.

Something seems to have gone wrong with our language. The implication of these two pieces of etymology is that hating children is such a universal characteristic that there is no need for a special word to describe it, and that loving children is such an impossibility that the only reason for apparently doing so must be sexual attraction. (The possibility that hating children is such a *rare* phenomenon that we have no need for a word to describe it is contradicted on the one hand by personal experience, and on the other by the existence of such words as photophobia, which means fear of light, and misocapnic, which means hating smoke.)

A xenophobe hates and is frightened of foreigners, an arachnophobe hates and is frightened of spiders, and I think we badly need the word paedophobe[3] for someone who hates and is frightened of children. Many of the objections cited in this chapter illustrate this need; perhaps the strongest indication is the enthusiastic way in which people embrace the notion of the *Lord of the Flies* syndrome.

One of the particularly disturbing things about paedophobia is the almost schizophrenic amnesia it implies. Not only does the typical paedophobe have no respect for children in general; he does not even have any respect for the child he himself once was.

---

3   Long after writing this, I came across the word "paedophobia" used repeatedly in a news report in the *Guardian*, 23 October 2006. It still had not reached Chambers Dictionary, but it was plainly on the way.

CHAPTER ELEVEN

MORE OBJECTIONS

Objection Ten

No educational philosopher, however concerned for the rights of children, has ever made the claim that children have a better moral understanding than adults. John Locke didn't, Rousseau didn't, Bertrand Russell didn't. It is absurd to go against such authorities.

Response

John Locke, as well as being a philosopher, was tutor to the Earl of Shaftesbury's children, and in 1693 wrote a book called *Some Thoughts Concerning Education*. He thought that children should be allowed a good deal of freedom, disapproved of the teaching of grammar, believed in reasoning with children, thought academic learning the least important part of education, recommended that punishment should be avoided if possible and thought the best way of teaching was to give children a "liking and inclination to what you propose to be learn'd." He put so much so well that I cannot resist quoting him.

Those children who have been most chastised, seldom make the best men.

Few years require but few laws.

It will perhaps be wondered, that I mention reasoning with children: and yet I cannot but think that this is the true way of dealing with them. They understand it as early as language.

Who is there that would not be disgusted with any innocent recreation, in itself indifferent to him, if he should with blows, or ill language, be hauled to it, when he had no mind?

... a father will do well, as his son grows up, and is capable of it, to talk familiarly with him; nay, ask his advice, and consult with him, about those things wherein he has any knowledge or understanding.

The native and untaught questions of inquisitive children do often offer things that may set a considering man's thought on work. And I think there is frequently more to be learned from the unexpected questions of a child, than from the discourses of men, who talk in a road, according to the notions they have borrowed, and the prejudices of their education.

If I mis-observe not they love to be treated as rational creatures sooner than is imagined.

All this seems to be little short of ideal, and all the more astonishing in that it was written in the seventeenth century, when the ordinary educational method was to beat every child who failed to learn, whether he, or she, for girls were beaten too, would not or could not. (Locke did favour beating in certain circumstances, and his idea of a beating was extremely severe, but he thought physical punishment was usually unnecessary as all action should be dictated by reason, and children respected reason as an element of maturity that they wished to acquire.)

However, these children, who love to be treated as rational creatures sooner than is imagined, nevertheless have to be taught to govern their desires, and we must make their minds "supple and pliant to what their parents' reason advises them now, and so prepare them to obey what their own reason shall advise hereafter." This is necessary because "the great principle and foundation of all virtue and worth is placed in this, that a man is able to deny himself his own desires, cross his own inclinations, and purely follow what reason directs as best, though the appetite lean the other way."

I would suggest that this demonisation of desire and inclination has the opposite results to those intended. Children whose minds have been made "supple and pliant to what their parents' reason advises" may well long to rebel, and for them virtue will be as heavy a burden as Locke implies. Children who have been brought up with a proper respect for their own intuitions, on the other hand, will find moral behaviour perfectly natural.

Rousseau, although regarded by some as the father of progressive education, actually had surprisingly little respect for the child. I have written about his book *Emile* in *Considering Children*, where I have explained my differences with him.

Bertrand Russell, as well as being a brilliant philosopher and mathematician, was a prominent figure in progressive education. He started Beacon Hill School with his wife, Dora, and later sent his children to Dartington Hall School. "Happiness in childhood is absolutely necessary to the production of the best type of human being," says Russell, and even though I am worried by the word 'production' I can agree with enthusiasm.

The following quotations are from his book *On Education*, published in 1926.

The spontaneous wish to learn, which every normal child possesses, as shown in its efforts to walk and talk, should be the driving-force in education. The substitution of this driving force for the rod is one of the great advances of our time.

Affection cannot be created, it can only be liberated.

Parents who wish to be loved must behave so as to elicit love.

We should be more concerned to produce sympathetic and affectionate adults than to force a precocious development of these qualities in early years.

If one can judge by the books of the old-fashioned disciplinarians, the children educated by the old methods were far naughtier than the modern child.

I agree with it all, though the awkward word 'produce' has cropped up again. On the other hand, I can also find plenty to disagree with:

... reaction against the old bad forms of discipline has tended to an undue laxity, which will have to give place to a new discipline, more internal and psychological than the old.

Every educated mother now-a-days knows such simple facts as the importance of feeding the infant at regular intervals, not whenever it cries. This practice has arisen because it is better for the child's digestion, which is an entirely sufficient reason. But it is also desirable from the point of view of moral education. Infants are far more cunning (not in the American sense) than grown-up people are apt to suppose; if they find that crying produces agreeable results, they will cry ... Unless the right methods are adopted in infancy, people in later life will be either discontented or grasping, according to the degree of their power. The right moment to begin the requisite moral training is the moment of birth.

The objectives of this moral training are to be vitality, courage, sensitiveness and intelligence. Sensitiveness has a rather special meaning – a combination of self-respect with a readiness to see other things as more important than self. The training is to be effected with the use of weapons (Russell's word) such as praise and blame and, very occasionally, punishment. This was never to include physical punishment, but Russell gives an unexpected account of how he accustomed his young son to sea-bathing after gentler methods had failed.

There was still a terror of going actually into the waves. After some unsuccessful coaxing, combined with the spectacle of everyone else bathing, we adopted old-fashioned methods. When he showed cowardice, we made him feel that we were ashamed of him; when he showed courage, we praised him warmly. Every day for about a fortnight, we plunged him up to the neck in the sea, in spite of his struggles and cries.

What has become plain is that Russell thought he knew what children needed to learn, and he was in fact prepared to use cruelty to enforce this learning. In his conclusion to the book his low opinion of the natural behaviour of a child is made absolutely clear. (The italics in the following extracts are mine.)

It is the business of early education to train the instincts so that they may produce a harmonious character, constructive rather than destructive, affectionate rather than sullen, courageous, frank and intelligent.

By *creating* the right habits and the right skill we *cause* the child's instincts themselves to prompt desirable habits.

When we have *created* young people freed from fear and inhibitions and rebellious or thwarted instincts, we shall open to them the world of knowledge, freely and completely.

Knowledge is the liberator from the empire of natural forces and destructive passions.

Russell, although he speaks elsewhere of "reverence for the child", plainly has no concept of the child's own values. "They are born with only reflexes and a few instincts," he says; "out of these, by the action of the environment, habits are produced which may be either healthy or morbid." Where does personality come from, then? Is it just a matter of habit? And what has happened to the spontaneous wish to learn? The action of the environment is important, because it is from the environment that the baby learns, but that is a very different idea from the notion of the environment as the active force.

Russell's approval of feeding the baby to a time-schedule, and not when it cries, is now happily out of date, but every mother who followed his advice must have suffered considerable distress herself (as my mother has told me that she did) and taught a strange lesson to her baby. "You cannot have what you want, you can only have what you are given. I do not love you enough to take your wishes into account." The consequence that might be expected from such a lesson is that when the baby grows up he or she will say to everyone else, "You cannot have what you want, you can only have what you are given. I do not love you enough to take your wishes into account." It does seem to be a common attitude among the middle-aged. Let us hope that those who have been treated more generously as babies will also behave more generously as adults. Even Russell's own justification of not feeding babies when they cry is peculiarly puritanical – "If they find that crying produces agreeable results, they will cry." He must believe that whatever is agreeable to the baby is also bad for it. Otherwise he would recognise this as an argument in favour of feeding on request.

Russell requires the child to be taught a number of virtues that arise naturally when there is no interruptive instruction. Affection does not need to be liberated if it has never been repressed. A sympathetic and affectionate adult develops naturally after a childhood full of sympathy and affection. Instincts produce harmonious character by natural interaction with other people; it is more natural to be constructive than destructive, affectionate than sullen. The risk of too much intervention is that you interfere with exactly those effects you are trying to achieve.

There is no need to create the right habits and the right skill. If they are right, the child will want to acquire them. You don't have to create young people freed from fear and inhibition, you only have to make sure they don't become subject to fear and inhibition in the first place. Knowledge is indeed a liberator, but "the empire of natural forces and destructive passions" is a chimera. The appalling wickednesses perpetrated in the name of religion and patriotism are the result of man's mistaken faith in the virtue of his own institutions; they are not natural at all.

Russell's willingness to leave his hungry babies to cry and to plunge his screaming son into the sea up to his neck every day for a fortnight, shows that he attached more importance to a set of values he had thought up for himself, than to the actual welfare of his children. He forced himself to behave unnaturally for the sake of his ideas, and in doing so he found himself behaving cruelly.

Children know, without having to be taught, that people are more important than ideas. Russell should have had more confidence in his observation of a child's desire to learn. What children need is not training, but affection, respect, opportunity, protection and encouragement.

Objection Eleven

Richard Dawkins has shown that it is impossible for altruism to evolve. Altruism must therefore be taught.

Response

Richard Dawkins' book *The Selfish Gene*, published in 1976, is a popularisation of a refinement of Darwin's theory of evolution. Richard Dawkins says that the phrase "survival of the fittest" should not be applied to the members of a species but to their genes. Genes he defines as genetic units "small enough to last for a large number of generations and to be distributed around in the form of many copies." Genes produce physical characteristics such as long tails or blue eyes, and behavioural patterns such as diving into water to catch fish, or caring for offspring. Genetic units this size are small enough to last, whereas large units, such as those required to make a particular individual, will not last for more than one generation. Some genes survive, and some die out. To give an example of my own, cows do not have a gene for diving into the water to catch fish because any cow who had it would drown and so not reproduce that gene. Genes and patterns of genes are not absolutely constant; although they are inherited, they are inherited from two different parents, so some of the patterns change. Genes that are unsuccessful in themselves, or unsuccessful in the company in which they find themselves, such as the diving gene in the cow, disappear. Successful genes multiply.

This seems unarguable. However, Dawkins adds a psychological element to the question, and there he begins to go wrong. These are his words:

Any gene which behaves in such a way as to increase its own survival chances in the gene pool at the expense of its alleles [other genes of the right configuration to fill the same position in the chromosome] will, by definition, tautologically, tend to survive. The gene is the basic unit of selfishness.

To ascribe selfishness to something that has no consciousness is an obvious absurdity, and Dawkins stresses that he is using the word metaphorically, but occasionally he switches to a literal use of the word without apparently being aware that he has made an illogical jump.

"A body is really a machine, blindly programmed by its selfish genes." This seems an adequate metaphor. "As a convenient approximation, we can once again assume that each individual body is a selfish machine, trying to do its best for all its genes." The selfishness has been transferred from the genes to the machine, which is not logically acceptable. Since the interests of the machine and the interests of the genes are not identical, the machine actually seems to be behaving unselfishly. However, Dawkins seems to think that he has proved that every living creature is selfish, in the literal sense, and says, "If there is a human moral to be drawn, it is that we must *teach* our children altruism, for we cannot expect it to be part of their biological nature."

There are at least two flaws in the argument – the transferring of the selfishness from the gene to the machine, and the switch from metaphorical to actual selfishness.

Dawkins also fails to recognise the possibility of two interpretations of a single event; this is evident in his accounts of altruistic behaviour on the part of animals.

Whales and dolphins drown if they are not allowed to breathe air. Baby whales, and injured individuals who cannot swim to the surface, have been seen to be rescued and held up by companions in the school. It is not known whether whales have ways of knowing who their close relatives are, but it is possible that it does not matter. It may be that the overall probability that a random member of the school is a relation is so high that the altruism is worth the cost.

Adult male baboons have been reported to risk their lives defending the rest of the troop against predators such as leopards. It is quite probable that any adult male has, on average, a fairly large number of genes tied up in other members of the troop. A gene which 'says', in effect: 'Body, if you happen to be an adult male, defend the troop against leopards', could become more numerous in the gene pool.

Yet according to Dawkins both actions are not really altruistic but selfish, because they result in the survival of the genes for such behaviour in other members of the same family. In the same way, the gene for pretending to have a broken wing and fluttering away from your nest when a fox comes past survives because even if the mother-bird gets caught, there is a good chance that her nestlings, who have the same gene, will survive.

The gene itself may be described as selfish; it is prepared to sacrifice even its host body so that exact replicas of itself may survive in other bodies. However, that does not make the action of the host body any less altruistic. All these behaviours can be explained in terms of 'selfish' genes, but they can also be described as altruism on the part of the animals created by those same genes. The two explanations are not incompatible.

This means that genes for altruistic behaviour do exist in animals, since Dawkins himself gives examples, such as the ones above. Although Dawkins has said that we cannot expect altruism to be part of our biological nature, in fact he has given evidence that we can.

Objection Twelve
Without rules we have no way of knowing how to behave.

Response

The American philosopher Lawrence Blum has answered this point much more effectively than I can.

In his book, *Friendship, Altruism and Morality*, he shows that altruistic emotion is usually a more effective guide to behaviour than any system of rules or duty. Even if the rules covered all moral action (which he shows they cannot do), then an insensitive person would not be able to tell when to apply them.

Charitable actions performed out of good will are more likely to be effective than the same actions performed from a sense of duty.

Rules do not change, but they do not necessarily lead to consistent behaviour, because our willingness to obey rules varies.

People whose lives are governed by rules are always having to make decisions and sacrifices; those whose lives are governed by altruistic emotion behave in a moral manner spontaneously and without regret.

Objection Thirteen

I found objection thirteen in an article in *The Tablet* in 1992 by John Patten, who was at that time Secretary of State for Education.

John Patten was a practising Roman Catholic who thought that the cause of the current increase in crime was not poverty or injustice or lack of opportunity but the loss of belief in hellfire.

In his article in *The Tablet*, however, he put forward a view of moral education which many non-religious people would find reasonable. He began by deploring our age as one in which "all views are taken as valid" and "there are doubts as to whether there are still values to which we should all subscribe." He then dismissed these doubts and went on to assert the importance of moral and spiritual development as part of the school curriculum. "The school's approach," he said, "should provide pupils with a clear and consistent set of values and opinions which later underpin the decisions which they face about their behaviour and the effect which their behaviour has on others," and, "We should not be apologetic about trying to instil in young people a sense of responsibility for their actions, respect and consideration for other people, respect for property, the values of honesty, trustworthiness, conscientiousness and fairness. Do not be afraid of the 'D' word, for discipline – self, school, community – makes our world bearable to live in." He also stressed the importance of example, and recognised that pupils value fairness.

After recommending religious education and collective worship as a means of developing in the children an understanding which will enable them to take decisions about their own lives, he observed that spiritual and moral values are not confined to those areas of the curriculum, but can crop up in music, literature, history or science. Although it might be easier to avoid moral issues in the classroom, in history, for example, children should be taught that although it "can at times seem a catalogue of evil perpetrated by the powerful on the weak ... the same event may equally be presented as the victory of right over wrong."

The surest way to virtue, though, is a religious upbringing. "Those with a secure foundation in faith have had guides from whom to learn, and clear signposts directing them. Children with parents who themselves hold religious beliefs will have support at home for the development of their own belief as well as enrichment at school – in spiritual terms, indeed, they have been spoiled rotten."

Response

I was brought up as a member of the Church of England, and for a long time I remained weakly attached to it, serious enough only to go to church at Christmas and occasionally take Holy Communion. I did not finally cease to do so until I was past fifty. I still feel a residual compulsion to believe what I am told in the name of religion, but nevertheless John Patten's attitude offends me.

How does he know that his moral code is the right one? I imagine the answer is that it comes from God. How then does he know that his is the right God? This question is blasphemous, impossible to entertain and therefore unanswerable. It is a matter of faith. He was taught his faith by his parents, and they knew. They knew because they had been taught by their parents. There can be no rational justification for faith in any religion. If there were a rational justification there would be no virtue in faith.

Children understand the difference between good and evil without reference to supernatural authority; if John Patten wishes to believe in a supernatural authority as well as the difference between good and evil of course he can, but there is no way to deduce the one from the other.

John Patten mentions doubt about whether there are values to which we should all subscribe. "Should" is an extraordinary word to have used. There are without doubt values to which we all *do* subscribe. He seems to have imagined a strange amoral society that he must somehow persuade that it "should", presumably for moral reasons, accept moral reasoning. Luckily he is not going to have to face this impossible task, because his original premise is wrong.

He then says that a school should provide its pupils with a set of values and opinions. Children arriving at a school for the first time may need to be provided with sets of geometrical instruments but they bring sets of values and opinions with them. The purpose of the school-provided set is said to be to underpin decisions about behaviour. The children have been making such decisions all their lives on the basis of their own personal sets. John Patten seems to believe that without guidance from their schools young people have no sense of responsibility for their actions, no consideration for other people and no respect for property, honesty, trustworthiness, conscientiousness or fairness. They need to have these things instilled into them.

In fact most children have all these things in abundance before they go to school, and most schools do a good deal to take them away. It is hard to hold on to your sense of responsibility for your own actions when all choice is taken from you, so that you are not even allowed the responsibility of choosing what colour of socks to wear. It is difficult to learn consideration for others from people who treat you without consideration.

Even John Patten finds himself acknowledging that pupils value fairness, so it is important for teachers to be fair. I wonder how he supposes children learn to recognise this quality.

He says that discipline is what makes our world bearable to live in. What a miserable man he must be! Is that the total purpose of moral behaviour, to make our world bearable to live in? Or have I completely misunderstood him? Did he just mean that we should not be afraid of disciplining children, because disciplining children makes our world bearable for adults? Surely someone writing about morality cannot have failed to reflect that discipline often makes the world unbearable for children.

In my last quotation from his article, Patten declares that a firm foundation in a religious faith is the best basis for sound moral development. His reason for believing this is that he had just such a firm foundation himself, but he is simply wrong. If a child's own opinions are always considered idle beside the commandments of God, the child will develop no judgement of his own, and will never grow beyond the stage of an irrational obedience to a set of rules. The way such a moral attitude can lead to catastrophic misjudgement is shown by Alice Miller's astonishing statistic about German terrorists that I quoted in Chapter Five – six out of ten were the children of Protestant clergy.

Objection Fourteen

Punishment has always been an essential element of society, because it is only through punishment that moral values can be inculcated and sustained.

Response

The fact that intelligent people can still believe in the notion that it is only the fear of punishment that keeps us from wrong-doing seems to me almost incredible. Even people who believe in the notion appear to understand that it is not fear of punishment that prevents them personally from lying or stealing, but they nevertheless believe that it is the only thing that holds other people back. Their assumption seems to be that they themselves are naturally good, but other people are bad unless they are afraid.

This assumption of moral superiority is a damaging start, but it is even worse that such people believe that their moral superiority gives them a right to punish others. It is true that fear of punishment can sometimes keep us from wrong-doing, but it can also keep us from harmless actions such as wearing red socks with our school uniforms, or, in a totalitarian regime, from virtuous actions such as going to the aid of the oppressed. Punishment is in itself an evil, since the intention of it is to make someone suffer. It is a tool, and can be used to various ends, but it is a tool that can only be used by the strong against the weak, and self-evidently lacks moral justification.

Without punishment, then, how are we to enforce the moral code?

The question has no meaning, because as soon as a moral code is enforced it ceases to be a moral code and becomes a set of conditioned reflexes. People act according to the moral code because they want to. It is simply not true that most people would commit rape and murder if they were not afraid of the law; nor would they get drunk and riot, or shoplift, or cheat, or neglect their children. It is a contradiction in terms to enforce a moral code. What we need to do instead is to respect each other's moral awareness, to acknowledge that morality is a part of human nature.

Obviously something has gone wrong when there is misbehaviour or crime, but punishment does not solve the problem, it adds to it.

Objection Fifteen

Surely teachers have a clearer idea of what children need to learn than the children themselves?

Children are born into the world entirely ignorant. Everything they need to learn has to be taught to them, either by their parents or by their schools. Moral behaviour has to be taught by instilling a number of rules.

Children come to school to learn. If they are not instructed in moral behaviour, they will have no basis on which to make moral decisions. You cannot expect children to behave well if they have never been told what good behaviour is.

Children like to be effectively organised. It is important for them to know exactly what to expect, and exactly how they are supposed to react. It gives them a sense of security, and allows them to concentrate on their studies.

Children need to learn to conform. Even wild individualists need to know what they are rejecting; all the rest of us need to know what is expected of us, and we do our best to fit in. The boy who insists on wearing red socks with his school uniform has to feel the full weight of society's disapproval, so that he learns the value of conformity. Society runs on the basis of rules and consensus. To refuse to accept the consensus is to outlaw yourself.

Most teachers have taken up teaching because they have a vocation; it is not a well-paid job or an easy one. They are people with high moral standards who understand that it is important that they should pass those moral standards on. They know the difference between right and wrong, and they have far wider experience than their pupils; what they must do is share their understanding with the children in their charge. If the children don't understand the message, then they must be obliged to behave as if they did, for whereas sound thinking is only a desirable accessory to the smooth running of a school, sound behaviour is essential.

A child's conscience is a primitive guide. The essential ingredient in a good moral education is a good teacher.

Response

I agree that children value order and clarity. As long as order is established by consent and not by domination it seems a desirable objective.

Of course teachers know more than children do, though not about everything. At the very least, children know more about their own states of health and states of mind and about their own social situations than their teachers do. If there is a difference of opinion as to whether these specialist areas of knowledge are more or less important than, say, the agreement of the past participle in verbs conjugated with être, which may happen to be part of the teacher's specialist area, I think I would probably come down on the child's side. When it comes to moral education, though, it is certainly the child's feelings and understanding that are central, and unless the teacher understands this nothing much can be learnt. In French grammar the driest of information is useful as long as it is understood; in moral education the richest of explanations is only of value if it is accepted.

Sound behaviour may make for a presentable atmosphere in a school, but to require sound behaviour without sound thinking behind it is to exercise your pupils in hypocrisy.

If children do not learn to conform at school they will not conform as adults, and, we are told, that will make life will be difficult for them. This is not moral education, it is education in self-interest. Conformity is not a virtue, it is a convenience. The desire to conform is often a reason for starting to smoke, drink and use drugs. Conformity is a close relation to racism, sexism, fascism, communism, every kind of -ism. Under its surface lie intolerance and fear of change.

The conventional teacher believes he knows what children should learn, and wants it to be taught effectively. His reason for this is that it is for the good of society. I think that education is for the good of the individual. He thinks that education for the good of the individual results in self-centredness. I think it results in a superior understanding which makes unselfishness a more likely outcome. He thinks society needs conformists in order to run smoothly. I think it needs individualists in order to develop. He likes rules. I like co-operation. His society depends on obedience. Mine depends on concern for other people. He thinks my ideas are Utopian and impractical. I think his ideas are pessimistic and wrong-headed.

What is more, I think his ideas, like John Patten's, are inherently inconsistent. John Patten's remark, "Discipline is what makes our world bearable to live in," implies its own refutation. Naturally we all agree that we want our world to be bearable to live in; it follows that there is no need for an externally imposed discipline.

Actually I don't believe that all we want is a world bearable to live in: I believe we want a world full of joy. We may not be going to get it, but it does seem a rather more worthwhile objective.

CHAPTER TWELVE

THE LIGHT OF COMMON DAY

The youth . . .
. . . by the vision splendid
Is on his way attended;
At length the man perceives it die away,
And fade into the light of common day.

William Wordsworth

Excuses for Not Bothering to Think

It is a commonly held view that we are driven primarily by self-interest, and that that self-interest is only held in check by the authority of the community. I have the impression that until about 1980 most psychologists regarded these ideas not as opinions but as facts.

Both halves of the view are wrong: we are not primarily driven by self-interest, and the voice of community, far from holding us in check, actually encourages us to do things that we would be ashamed to do if we did not have such encouragement. As we grow older and become more deeply involved in society, so we find moral decisions more and more often made for us by institutions or groups that we belong to, and our behaviour becomes increasingly irresponsible. This does not go unnoticed by children. As Cedric Cullingford reports in *Children and Society*, "Children in school think rules are extremely important, and actually assume that they become more important as people become older, since the older people are the more they are inclined to depravity." In this chapter I shall point to some of the ways in which society encourages this inclination, while the individual tries to resist it.

Society has two main ways of supposedly encouraging moral behaviour – religion and the law. Neither has anything like the effect attributed to it.

Religion

Of course there are good people who associate their goodness with their religion, and of course there are Christian moral injunctions of the highest kind. (In talking of religion I shall have to refer to the only one I know a certain amount about, having worshipped willingly even though under compulsion fourteen times a week all through school terms from the age of 13 to the age of 18.) I can see that religion and virtue are often comfortable companions, but I do not believe that the one is the root of the other. What we take from religion is not what it requires us to take, but simply what we choose.

The ten commandments are still often cited as a source of moral authority. You shall have no other gods but me. You shall not make yourself a graven image. You shall not take the name of the Lord your God in vain. Remember the Sabbath day and keep it holy. Honour your father and mother. You shall not kill, commit adultery, steal or bear false witness against your neighbour. You shall not covet anything that is your neighbour's. How many of those would come in any modern person's top ten moral rules for their own behaviour? When Channel 4 polled their viewers in 2005 for the commandments they would favour today, only four of the orginal ten made the top twenty. Those four were, in the words of the programme, don't kill, don't steal, respect your mother and father, and don't commit adultery. More important than any of these were, treat others as you would like to be treated, take responsibility for your own actions, be honest and protect and nurture children. The top of the list, "Treat others as you would like to be treated," was expressed more eloquently by Jesus – "Love thy neighbour as thyself" – but that was not one of the original ten.

Some years previously I had asked a group of thirteen-year-olds to think what they would put down as the most important commandments for themselves. This is one girl's list:-

Love your work.

Look happy at your past and look to your future.

Never let yourself down.

Never accuse when you're not sure.

Think positive.

Help anyone who needs it.

You are not forced to do things, but do them when they are needed.

There is an underlying assumption that anyone will know what is "needed". There is no point in spelling out the detail.

The sequel to the original ten commandments in the Bible is rather surprising. After a short narrative passage with thunder and lightning, a smoking mountain and trembling people, the Lord delivers a whole lot more instructions to Moses. You shall not make gods of silver or gold. You shall make an altar of earth and sacrifice sheep and oxen. You shall not make an altar of hewn stone. You shall not go up to my altar by steps.

After this curiously incomplete guide to worship, which contains three prohibitions to one command, there follow three chapters of laws. Many of these concern slaves. If, after six year's service, your slave is married to one of your female slaves and says, "I love my master, my wife and my children; I will not go out free," then you should take him to a door or door-post, and bore through his ear with an awl. He is then your slave for life.

Why do we choose to respect the first ten commandments, but not the next ten? It may be possible to produce some intellectual wriggles and escape from this question, but it seems likely that the reason we ignore the next ten is that we do not like them. Animal sacrifice and slavery are no longer acceptable to us.

Further down the list there are commandments that are ignored for the opposite reason – that they ask too much of us.

If you lend money to any of my people with you who is poor, you shall not be to him as a creditor, and you shall not exact interest from him. (*Exodus*, 22.25)

If ever you take your neighbour's garment in pledge, you shall restore it to him before the sun goes down; for that is his only covering, it is his mantle for his body, in what else shall he sleep? (22.26–27)

If you meet your enemy's ox or his ass going astray, you shall bring it back to him. (23.4)

For six years you shall sow your land and gather in its yield; but the seventh you shall let it rest and lie fallow, that the poor of your people may eat, and what they leave the wild beasts may eat. You shall do likewise with your vineyard, and with your olive orchard. (23.10–11)

Christians have an excuse for not letting the poor have all the fruit their gardens produce once every seven years. This is only required by the Old Testament. It's difficult for Jews, but Christians only have to do what it says in the New Testament. Oh yes. What Christians have to do is sell all that they have and give to the poor, turn the other cheek if anyone strikes them, love their enemies and chop off their own hands if they are tempted to do evil. Things like that.

Most people who say they are Christians simply choose which aspects of Christ's teaching they want to accept. Some of them object to the idea of a man being cast into outer darkness where there shall be weeping and gnashing of teeth merely because he turned up at a wedding in the wrong clothes. Others are sure that rich men can get into the kingdom of heaven much more easily than a camel can get through the eye of a needle, and claim to have discovered that "The Eye of a Needle" was the popular name for a narrow gate in Jerusalem. John Robinson, the Bishop of Woolwich famous for his book *Honest to God*, says this about the Sermon on the Mount:

> Regarded as a code of conduct, prescribing what one should do in any situation, the Sermon on the Mount is quite impracticable. It tears the individual loose from any horizontal nexus. In any given precept it rules out of consideration all other interests, all other values, all other people. It never weighs conflicting responsibilities or helps a man to balance his commitments. It simply says, "Give to him who asks you", with never a thought for the stewardship of money. It commends the widow who throws "all her livelihood" into the treasury without asking who is to support her henceforth. It does not take into account – it does not reckon to take into account – the fact that there is always more than one neighbour to be considered, always more than one claim upon one. (*Christian Morals Today, SCM Broadsheet*)

The bishop was considered outrageously radical in the 1960s, but he still strives to make a case for conservative financial values. He even makes the transparent error of suggesting that if you have more than one claim on you it becomes unreasonable to expect you to meet even one of them. Surely the more neighbours there are to be considered, the stronger the case for divesting yourself of your wealth.

John Patten, one-time Minister of Education, favours the use of the fear of hellfire to persuade people to behave as he thinks they should. Margaret Thatcher thinks "Love thy neighbour as thyself" means "Hate thy neighbour if thou disapproveth of him." In *The Lord of the Flies* it is the choir-boy who leads the savages. The best and kindest people I know are most of them agnostics. They don't have to find support for their views in the Bible; they have confidence in their own judgement. One of the differences between them and over-zealous religious people is that they are more tolerant of others and readier to recognise merit in them. Religion is no guarantee of virtue. Christianity has been used as a justification for atrocities, for instance in the Crusades, or the Inquisition, or more recently in Northern Ireland.

We are safer with people whose moral values do not depend on religion.

The Law

We are also safer with people whose moral attitudes do not depend on the law. The law purports to be about restricting the behaviour of villains, but it is more often about permitting behaviour that many people would otherwise consider impermissible.

The *British Social Attitudes* report for 1991 included a survey of opinions about business morality by Professor Michael Johnston of Colgate University, NY. In one part of the survey respondents were presented with sixteen instances of dubious ethical behaviour, and were asked to rate them as not wrong, a bit wrong, wrong, seriously wrong or very seriously wrong. These are the situations:

1. An employee uses his influence to get a relative a job at his workplace.

2. A company manager accepts a Christmas present worth £75 from a firm from which he buys products.

3. A householder is having a repair job done by a local plumber. He is told that if he pays cash he will not be charged VAT; so he pays cash.

4. A factory discovers it is polluting a river and does nothing about it.

5. A drug company delays supplies of an important new drug in order to keep its price high.

6. A lawyer is told by a client that the client's firm is about to announce big profits. The lawyer buys shares in the firm before the announcement is made.

7. A milkman slightly overcharges customers over a period and makes £300.

8. A company director makes a habit of taking time off as sick leave when he is not ill.

9. A company employee exaggerates his claims for travel expenses over a period and makes £75.

10. In making an insurance claim a man whose home has been burgled exaggerates the value of what was stolen by £150.

11.   A man gives a £5 note for goods in a big store and is given change for a £10 note by mistake. He notices but keeps the change.

12.   A British firm competing for a contract in a foreign country offers large gifts of money to officials.

13.   A tobacco manufacturer sponsors a national event popular with young people to get publicity.

14.   Two large breweries agree to raise their prices at the same time.

15.   A company provides its directors with expensive company cars even though they are rarely used for work.

16.   A private taxi firm puts up its fares during a public transport strike.

It is worth thinking for a moment how you would rate these actions yourself. In my opinion, for instance, there is nothing wrong with number one, and not much wrong with number two. However, the results of the survey show that every example was rated at least a bit wrong by more than half the respondents, and if you exclude the first three examples from the list, even the least disapproved of was still condemned by five out of six people. The polluting factory was disapproved of by everybody, and the drug company, the milkman and the malingerer were all disapproved of by ninety-nine people out of a hundred. In every case from number four onwards, the majority of people considered the behaviour described either wrong, seriously wrong or very seriously wrong.

The point of going on about this at such length is that quite a large number of the actions described are not in fact against the law. This includes the drug delay, which was rated by the respondents to be the second-worst example, less wrong only than the pollution by the factory. Someone who was controlled entirely by the law, and only by the law, would find nothing wrong with items 1, 2, 5, 13 and 16, and would only be mildly bothered about items 11 and 15. In these cases at least, the individual conscience is stricter than the law.

		Nothing wrong	A bit wrong	Wrong	Seriously wrong	V. seriously wrong
1.	Nepotism	44	22	24	5	3
2.	Taking gift	33	20	31	10	4
3.	Evading VAT	27	28	36	5	3
4.	Pollution	0	0.5	9	30	60
5.	Drug delay	0	12	26	33	38
6.	Insider deal	5	6	29	29	29
7.	Milkman	0.5	2	26	43	28
8.	Malingerer	0	14	34	37	24
9.	Fiddling expenses	3	15	50	21	10
10.	Overclaiming	6	20	55	13	5
11.	Keeping change	8	15	59	11	6
12.	Company gifts	7	10	33	28	20
13.	Tobacco sponsor	16	11	33	19	19
14.	Brewers' Cartel	17	10	36	20	14
15.	Company cars	13	11	40	21	13
16.	Taxi fares	7	13	42	25	12

I have quoted these examples because they are supported by statistical evidence, but we do not need statistics to tell us that on the one hand it is not merely the law that keeps us from theft and murder, and on the other there are no laws enjoining friendliness, generosity or patience. Nor do we need statistics to tell us that we will sometimes do things that we consider wrong, just as we will sometimes do things that are against the law.

We are obliged by law to pay taxes, and we pay them reluctantly, but we accept that they are a necessary cost of our society. We are also obliged by law to observe speed-limits, yet most of us frequently ignore them. In this case the law has some effect, but it does not restrain us all the time. A more immediate understanding of the cost of our speeding in terms of human suffering would have some effect, but a general renunciation of speeding and condemnation by all our friends would almost certainly succeed. The need to conform is more powerful than the law.

Conformity

By far the strongest observable influences on our moral behaviour are our own personal convictions and the opinions of our families, friends and acquaintances. Agreement with particular religious injunctions and obedience to particular laws are either personal decisions or else evidence of a ready acceptance of what other people around seem to accept. It is easy to break the law with a bunch of approving friends by, for instance, smoking a joint, and it is difficult to make a stand if you disapprove of cannabis but all your friends are telling you it doesn't matter – telling you, for instance, to relax and enjoy yourself. Condemning something as "a bit wrong" or "wrong", as the respondents to the *British Social Attitudes* survey did, does not mean that you will never do it, and if all your friends want you to do something that you consider only "a bit wrong" then the ties of friendship are likely to be more important to you than moral considerations.

Nevertheless, expectations of friends and family generally include at the least considerate behaviour, loyalty, honesty and affection, and often go very much further. This visible influence is generally a good one. It is the invisible influences that lead to most cruelty and unhappiness. I shall suggest that these influences do not stem from any moral principles, but only originate from the various institutions our society has created; nevertheless we have accepted them as inevitable.

Institutions

"The highest triumph of institutional thinking is to render the institution completely invisible," says Mary Douglas in *How Institutions Think*.

It is like an inversion of Hans Andersen's story of the emperor's new clothes. Everyone knows a rough outline of the story, but there are some details that are worth recalling. The weavers persuaded the emperor that they were making him a wonderful suit of clothes that was invisible to anyone *who was not fit for the office he held, or who was impossibly stupid*. The emperor of course could not admit that he couldn't see these clothes, and when in consequence he took part in a procession stark naked, no one else dared admit not being able to see them either. Eventually a small child pointed out that the emperor had nothing on. Even then the people hesitated, but soon everybody realised it was true. The emperor writhed, because he knew it was true too, but he thought, "The procession must go on now", and he drew himself up with more dignity than ever, and the pages behind him went on holding up the non-existent train.

Our position is not that we are naked when we think we are clothed, but that we are shackled when we think we are free. Invisible institutions have dressed us in invisible chains. Unfortunately when a child asks us why we are wearing these shackles and chains we deny that they exist. In our story the magic really works.

These are the names of some of the chains: civil order, freedom of movement, education, justice, good business practice, defence of the nation, free trade, Western values.

In the name of civil order, we victimise gypsies and travellers.

In the name of freedom of movement, roads are built where thousands of us are killed every year.

In the name of education a noticeable proportion of our children are subjected to lives of almost intolerable misery.

In the name of justice women have their families taken from them, lose their right to their homes and are sent to prison because they have not got enough money to pay for their television licences.

In the name of good business practice profits and dividends are considered more important than service.

In the name of defence of the nation millions of pounds are spent on weapons of insane destruction.

In the name of free trade, we sell these weapons to our enemies.

In the name of Western values, whole nations are broken apart by war.

Unless you see some of these examples as either acceptable or inevitable then my point has not been made. The chains that bind us really are invisible; we really do not see them.

Alan Clark, a former minister of the British government, was able to say that war between Iraq and Iran was in the British interest, because of the increased trade in arms. What horrifies me is not only that he was able to say it, but also that he expected his reasoning to be widely accepted, and what is still more horrifying is that it apparently was. It is difficult not to launch into a tirade like an Old Testament prophet; it seems incredible that such wickedness can go uncondemned.

These things are not done by individuals, they are done by institutions. Even Alan Clark would probably not have encouraged his neighbours to fight a duel just because he had pistols to sell to them. They are done by institutions, and the institutions are so vast and so all-pervasive that they seem an essential part of our background.

Institutions are made up of individuals, but the individuals are powerless against them. In a war which no one wants to fight, people will kill and maim others who were once their friends. The police are obliged to enforce laws and government decisions with which they may well not be in agreement. Desperate teachers make desperate children more desperate by punishing them. Because the best job a man can get is making bombs, he makes bombs.

The gulf between individual and institutional morality is shown by the support for Oxfam, the enormous response to the television charity events and the generosity to victims of disasters.

Governments and the Public

Very occasionally public protest actually manages to influence government action.

In the United States a change in public opinion led the end of the Vietnam war.

In Britain in 1992 Michael Heseltine announced the proposed closure of thirty-one coal-pits, and the redundancy of thirty thousand miners. There was enormous indignation on a national scale, among all economic groups. The government insisted that there was an unanswerable case for closing the thirty-one pits, but when faced with defeat in parliament, climbed down, at least temporarily, and agreed to set up an enquiry into the viability of the British coal industry.

This enquiry side-stepped the moral issue that had concerned the

British public, which was horror at the wilful imposition of unemployment and the destruction of the mining communities. Arguments arose about relative prices of coal, gas and oil, national assets, independence from other countries, the subsidising of nuclear power, mistakes in the privatisation of electricity and so on. The arguments were returned to the institutional plane where the sacking of thirty thousand men needs only the stroke of a pen to justify it. Concern for the miners themselves was forgotten. The closing of the pits was only postponed.

The poll tax riots in London, along with large-scale refusal to pay the tax, played a large role in the fall of Margaret Thatcher. On the other hand, the huge protests against the invasion of Iraq in 2003 were high-handedly ignored.

Stephen Plowden, the transport expert, has been painstakingly pointing out the absurdity of British road-building programmes for more than a quarter of a century, but there was no political reaction until the road-protesters began to gain publicity by spectacular direct action. Even so the road lobby, with all the resources of the big lorry and engineering companies behind it, is still generally more powerful than reason.

Recent protests have been unusual in that they have involved all age-groups in a common moral concern. As we get older, we become more and more closely identified with our national institutions, and more and more strongly influenced by them. Usually protesters are young, and usually the older generation disapproves of the protest.

By the time we are middle-aged most of us accept the institutional views as inevitable, and are prepared to go along with the evictions and the sackings and the imprisonment and the armaments and the wars that our institutions demand. Our moral sensitivity has been blunted, and we find it easier to conform than to object. We do not recognise the wrong that we do.

Crime and Age

Most crime is committed by young people. Joy-riding, breaking and entering, vandalism, mugging are all primarily activities of the young. Older people commit fewer crimes, but the crimes they commit tend to be far more serious — embezzlement, fraud, tax evasion, murder. Apart from murder, these crimes have a strange sort of respectability, because they are committed from behind a desk, but those responsible for the collapse of BCCI or Robert Maxwell's raiding of the Mirror Group pension funds caused far more serious suffering than burglars do.

Self-imposed disasters, such as divorce or alcoholism, are commoner among older people, and cause more suffering than the promiscuity or drug-use that might be considered to be the corresponding failings of the young adult. Poverty, vagrancy and prostitution are disasters created by society, not by individuals. Society teaches itself to tolerate them by cultivating either indifference, hostility or blindness.

The older we get, the more ready we are to accept conformity as our guide rather than our own real perceptions of right and wrong. There is no difficulty about the proper meaning of the words: right means likely to increase happiness or diminish suffering and wrong means likely to diminish happiness or increase suffering. There can be arguments about whether certain actions are right or wrong, but none about the meaning of the words. Happiness and suffering, right and wrong, are not things that we have to have explained to us. They are observable without instruction.

The enormous amount of evil at large in the world, almost entirely unrecognised, passing as it does for economic necessity, political caution and so on, is accepted because we have allowed our natural understanding of right and wrong to be overridden by concern for the preservation of our institutions. Because we are too old to believe in our own virtue, we believe we have to force ourselves to conform by obeying laws and conventions. We deliberately bind ourselves back into the conventional stages of moral development, those of conformity and irrational-conscientiousness, but these habits of mind actually contribute to, or even entirely cause, the greater part of man-made suffering. They are not truly moral positions at all, but at best amoral and all too often outright immoral.

People form themselves into groups for their mutual benefit, but as soon as a group is formed, it assumes an identity of its own, and struggles to survive. Very soon the survival of the group is seen as more important than the welfare of its individual members. This seems to be the basic fault of all institutions.

The Naturalness of Altruism

A few lines earlier I wrote that we believe we have to force ourselves to conform. This idea that virtue can only be achieved by an effort of will is due to a catastrophic misunderstanding of the nature of altruism. Altruism does not mean sacrificing your own happiness so that others can be happy. It means understanding that your own happiness is greater when others are happy too.

Lawrence Blum puts a similar point of view somewhat more cautiously:

> By 'altruism' I will mean a regard for the good of another person for his own sake, or conduct motivated by such a regard ... it departs from ordinary use in not carrying the connotation of self-sacrifice, or, at least, self-neglect ... in my usage, to say that an act is altruistic is only to say that it involves and is motivated by a genuine regard for another's welfare; it is not to say that in performing it the agent neglects his own interests and desires.

The people who sacrifice themselves are slaves to their irrational consciences, unnecessarily martyred, or slaves to conformity, marching off to be slaughtered in a battle. In our conventional education system and the models of behaviour we offer, everything society does to children tends to build up conformity and irrational obedience, but these are, as I have shown, profoundly dangerous tendencies. At best all they can do is contain the behaviour of people who have had every true moral consideration educated out of them; at worst they can compel torture and genocide. The belief in their necessity is the result of an infinite cynicism about human nature, an insane terror of what one might do oneself if one were not restrained. (This terror is a self-evident absurdity, for if one's fundamental desires were really evil, freedom from restraint would not be a terror but an orgiastic delight.)

Our fear of the supposed evil within ourselves is no more sensible than agoraphobia or a fear of spiders, but it is more dangerous because it is generally regarded as completely reasonable. We believe we have to subject our passions to our will. The evil that we fear is nothing more nor less than the selfish desires which John Locke so feared, and which almost all psychologists used to believe to be the sole driving force of our behaviour.

Mary Douglas thinks that this situation has been created on purpose.

> Only by deliberate bias and by an extraordinarily disciplined effort has it been possible to erect a theory of human behaviour whose formal account of reasoning only considers the self-regarding motives, and a theory that has no possible way of including community-mindedness or altruism, still less heroism. (*How Institutions Think*)

Children have not yet been affected by such a theory of human behaviour. When they read fiction they identify with the goodies and not the baddies. No one reading Harry Potter is on the side of Voldemort. Children still want to be community-minded, altruistic, even heroic. As they grow older, they learn that society expects otherwise.

CHAPTER THIRTEEN

THOU BEST PHILOSOPHER

Thou, whose exterior semblance doth belie
    Thy soul's immensity;
Thou best philosopher, who yet dost keep
Thy heritage, thou Eye among the blind.

William Wordsworth

Origins of Children's Morality

When a baby girl is born she cannot distinguish between her body and the rest of the world. Her own fingers are no more controllable than her mother's breast. Gradually she learns her own boundaries, and finds out how to control her limbs. She discovers that some of the things she can see are part of her, and some are independent. The physical separateness of her body from the rest of the world becomes apparent to her.

Psychic separation comes later. In Chapter One I quoted Osbert Sitwell's memory of feeling himself at one with his surroundings at the age of four. I don't see how it could be proved that this feeling of unity with the material world is common in early childhood, but a feeling of unity with other people is observably the norm. The mutual pleasure of mother and baby during feeding is only the first stage of it. The fact that babies are affected by each other's crying is well-documented, and in a crèche the presence of one unhappy child can cause distress to the whole group.

Small children's empathy was in fact professionally recorded by psychologists as early as 1937, but little attention has been paid to it. Martin L. Hoffmann, writing in Thomas Lickona's book, *Moral Development and Behaviour*, published in 1976, says this:

> The tendency to respond empathically to another in distress has long been noted in children and adults. Murphy (1937, p. 295) in her classic study described numerous instances of empathic responses in nursery school children and concluded that 'experiencing distress when another is in distress seems primitive, naive, reasonably universal.'

There used to be a tendency to explain these phenomena as mechanical reflexes with no moral content. I could not accept that explanation, and was pleased to find my opinion was shared by Bertrand Russell. Here are two of his anecdotes illustrating his point of view:

> Children are worried when their brothers or sisters cry, and often cry too. They will take their part vehemently against the grown-ups when disagreeable things are being done to them. When my boy had a wound in his elbow which had to be dressed, his sister (aged 18 months) could hear him crying in another room, and was very much upset. She kept on repeating "Jonny crying, Jonny crying", until the painful business was finished.

> When my boy saw his mother extracting a thorn with a needle from her foot, he said anxiously, "It doesn't hurt, mummy." She said it did, wishing to give him a lesson in not making a fuss. He insisted that it didn't hurt, whereon she insisted that it did. He then burst into sobs just as vehement as if it had been his own foot.

I remember my sister falling into a pond when she was about nine and I was about six. She jumped up in the water and shrieked with laughter, and I cried because I was so concerned about her. In a dormitory of nine-year-olds at my prep-school there was a peculiar instance of physical sympathy when one boy threw up in the night and a second promptly threw up too, not because he was ill or because he was disgusted, but because he completely shared the first boy's physical sensations.

In Chapter Two I quoted Eric Gill describing the horror he felt when his mother did not understand his innocence in some trivial matter. I suggest that the horror was a consequence of a belief that his mother ought to be able to look into his mind as he felt he could look into hers.

James Kirkup, in his autobiographical book *Sorrows, Passions and Alarms*, described how he understood his parents' emotions when his father, against his mother's wishes, threw some old, unwanted toys, boxes and shoes into the fire.

> I could see my mother's point of view. I was sometimes alarmed by the extent to which I could enter into the moods and thoughts of others. Often I would take her side, and we would enjoy using our concentrated efforts to try to restrain my father's outbursts. I think in this case I was more in sympathy with my father, but I understood the feelings of both with an almost painful clarity.

Support from Psychology

Psychological research has produced other results confirming this kind of sensitivity. Candida C. Peterson wrote a relevant paper about lying which was published in *Children's Interpersonal Trust*, edited by Ken J. Rotenberg.

Her paper reminds us that Piaget thought children had no moral discrimination up to the age of at least ten. His finding was that children up to the age of ten judged a lie to be an incorrect statement, whether there was any intention to deceive or not. However, more recent research with children between the ages of four and six has shown that in fact they do base their moral evaluations on the speaker's intention to speak honestly or deceptively. But not always.

When the consequences of a lie, however, are depicted in another way, as material damage, a very different pattern of empirical results emerges. In his original study, Piaget (1932) included a pairwise contrast between a deliberate lie that resulted in material help (a lost tourist found his way despite the liar's intention to misdirect him) versus an unintentional deception that resulted in material harm (the tourist got lost). He found that most children under the age of 9 or 10 judged the harmful accidental lie as the naughtiest. This finding has been replicated using different stories of similar format by Boehm and Nass (1962), Lickona (1976) and Peterson et al. (1983). In other words, there is evidence of moral realism when children are asked to judge lies whose consequences are materially damaging rather than more or less literally true ... results like these support Piaget's suggestion that the material harm caused by a lie is a more salient moral issue to young children than the liar's subjective intentions.

The phrase "moral realism" in this context means condemning an incorrect statement as a lie even when it was made in good faith. A lie, so defined, that is to say simply an incorrect statement, is seen by children as worse if it has damaging consequences than if it causes no harm. This view is exactly in line with the view of Vivian Gussin Paley's nursery group from Chicago, described in Chapter Three: what matters to the children is that everyone should be happy, or if that is unachievable that they should suffer as little as possible; abstract issues such as honesty take a second place.

Nevertheless, though honesty may come second, it does have a place. Peterson's research and the research of Kim in South Korea, published in 1986, showed that children as young as five gave harsher moral ratings to deliberate lies told for personal gain than to lies told for altruistic reasons.

Magda Stouthamer-Loeber, in another paper in *Children's Interpersonal Trust*, commented that children younger than five have more moral understanding than previously thought, and showed a number of unexpected capabilities.

Many of these capabilities seem to be related to children's ability to anticipate and act on the knowledge of another person's feelings and probable reactions. Examples of these capabilities are role-playing, empathy and altruism.

My suggested explanation of Eric Gill's horror at his mother's lack of understanding fits in well with this finding.

A Sense of Unity

What all this means is that though babies soon learn to distinguish their bodies from other people's, they continue to share the feelings of other people for very much longer, and for a young child another person's happiness or pain can be as important as her own.

Most of us, as adults, have few memories of such sympathy as small children, but we may have experienced something similar when we were in love, and were more concerned for the welfare of our loved one than for our own. Or perhaps we remember, as parents, having a similar intensity of love for our children. It seems that at times young children love many people in that way, possibly all their acquaintances. They don't do so all the time, because there are times when they pull their hair and take their toys, but they are capable of such feeling.

Homesickness – which should really be called parentsickness because it is the absence of parents that is so distressing – has actual physical manifestations such as loss of appetite, listlessness and insomnia; lovesickness has the same symptoms. Children show a devotion to other people that in adults is usually only associated with falling in love. As with the adults, this devotion is not a deliberately chosen moral course, but a spontaneous identification with the other person's interests, a feeling that they and their partners in this behaviour – their parents, their friends, their lovers, or other people in general – are in some way profoundly unified. The difference between adults and children is that for a child this is often not just a feeling but a self-evident truth.

Attitude to Justice

The children's attitude to justice in Vivian Gussin Paley's nursery group shows how other people's welfare is the most important issue for them. Earl will be happy as long as someone makes him a new house, so there is no point in punishing Eddie who broke the old one. When Tanya keeps interrupting the record that Jill is listening to, Jill agrees to change the record to one that they both enjoy. Eddie and Tanya have behaved badly because they are unhappy. Punishment is pointless because it creates more unhappiness. The culprit needs to be cared for just as much as the victim.

I met a different attitude in an adult who was objecting to the fact that there was no system of punishment at Sands School. I asked her why she thought punishment was necessary, and by way of illustration she described two instances of her own punitive behaviour when looking after a young nephew and niece. On the first occasion the boy pulled the girl's hair, so the adult pulled the boy's hair, partly, she said, to make him let go, partly as a punishment and partly to show him what it was like. On the next occasion the boy had hit the girl, so the woman caught him tightly in her arms and invited the girl to hit him back. The girl refused to do so. It might possibly be necessary to remind a young child that having one's hair pulled is painful, though it seems unlikely that he did not know. The girl seems to be the only person to come out of this with any credit. She was concerned for general welfare while both the boy and the woman gave way to violence. Although the boy had behaved badly, the moral score was still children 1, adults 0.

Cedric Cullingford, in *Children and Society*, comments on the fact that junior-school children do not automatically associate law and morality, and that in school they see rules as sanctions imposed on them rather than agreed social necessities. Rules and laws naturally seem superficial if you see all morality as based on a deeply felt concern for other people.

Rules are the first step in the domination of the individual conscience by social institutions.

The Consequences of Two Crimes

Just before I was nine I was sent to a boarding-school where we were regimented perhaps a little less than in many other prep-schools at that time. Nevertheless it was extremely like Linbury Court, the school Anthony Buckeridge created in the Jennings books.

In spite of being transparently determined to behave as well as possible,

I was caned. The first time it happened in the dining-room. I had to stand at the end of a table and then bend over so my face rested on the pale brown oak. I had to hold on to the side of the table. I can remember the swish of the cane, and I think I remember being astonished at the sharpness of the pain. You had to concentrate above all on *not crying*; the important thing was not to cry. I don't remember how many strokes I had, but I think it was three or four. When I went back to my classroom people laughed at me because I was cautious about sitting down.

What I don't remember is what I was being caned for.

This is very different from John Burningham's experience at Summerhill with its headmaster, A.S. Neill. John Burningham and a friend slept in an old railway carriage in the grounds; they had got hold of the key to the food store, and this is his account of what happened.

For what seemed like weeks we revelled in an orgy of late-night consumption of tinned fruit and Carnation milk. I used to throw the empties out of the railway carriage window into the bushes behind. It reached a point where it was hard to throw a can out without hitting another one.

But the day of reckoning had to come. I was visiting Neill's house for reasons I now forget. I found him in his sitting room, buried behind a newspaper and only his large boots were visible.

"Some bugger has got the key to the store room, Brum," he said from behind the paper. "You wouldn't happen to know who that is would you?" I left immediately and returned, minutes later, with the key. A hand emerged from one side of the paper and took it. "Thank you very much," said Neill and continued to read. I departed.

This experience has stayed with me... Neill gave me freedom and a chance to develop my own framework of belief. Certainly, it was my last sortie into organised crime and nowadays I find it hard to even throw a matchstick out of a car window.

'Heroes and Villains', in *The Independent*, November 7, 1992

For Neill, John Burningham's natural honesty was self-evident in spite of his crime. Neill's recognition of this honesty was enough to alter

Burningham's whole behaviour. My headmaster, however, had quite failed to recognise my natural good intentions and he inflicted a punishment that seems to have been completely pointless because I can't remember what I was supposed to have done wrong.

Punishments nowadays are less savage, but the contrast between the effects of punishment and the effects of trust holds good. "It is better to trust and be deceived than to suspect and be mistaken," said someone whose remark I copied into a notebook without recording the source. A lack of adult trust undermines children's confidence in their own judgement and tends to make them depend on what they are told rather than what they know. E. M. Forster expressed the same idea in *Howard's End*. These are the words of Helen Schlegel, speaking about her father:

> "You remember how he would trust strangers, and if they fooled him he would say, 'It is better to be fooled than to be suspicious' – that the confidence trick is the work of man, but the want-of-confidence trick is the work of the devil."

Mai-Bente

The events surrounding the International Children's Hearing (Chapter Eight) produced many examples of young people's clarity of moral perception, but one of the most striking was the reaction of the Norwegian girl, Mai-Bente, to the slums of Rio. She spoke about her experiences to Sarah McCrum. The conversation was recorded on tape.

Mai-Bente: At first I came. I saw these boys sniffing glue and smoking something they were holding and oh, I felt it really was – I've never seen such things before, because it's very little of that in my town. And I went up and saw these rivers of just shit, you know, I felt really sick. You have to see it before you can just tell it, because you feel so much inside you.

I go through this little rooms between the house, and I saw this little kid stand in the door and look at me and just smile. I was so – just – as I came there as a rich person, you know.

And I went up and I saw this market or something. I don't know how to – a little shop with a butcher, and this meat hanging and a lot of insects and all things, and it – oh it was really disgusting.

Sarah: Did you think you were rich before you went there?

Mai-Bente: No. I felt like a normally poor person, not rich, not poor, and just in the middle. I have clothes every day, I have something to wear, I have food every day, I have a big house, like everyone else of my friends. I didn't feel like that, but when I came there I felt like a really rich person.

I felt that – think about if I had given them some of my things, if we had not this big house – we have 3 floors in our house and I thought they haven't got anything called a house. They've just got this paper bag – and I felt so guilty because I have all this, they have nothing.

Every day I go to school, and I've got good clothes, and stand up and my mother is smiling to me and giving me food, and I have this, and she hugs me and I really feel good. And I go home from school and get dinner and I go to sleep and have a good day.

I'm doing with sport and all that kind – they have this garbage and they are playing football. I felt, I don't know how they could live there. I couldn't. Oh, they are used to it, but they are happy to have this.

Sarah: How did they seem to be as people to you?

Mai-Bente: Oh, just like me. With feelings and like – just like me.

They haven't got the material things like I have, but they've got feelings, they feel the same as me. And they just smiled to me and they were happy because they have this thing to live in.

I came here and I went shopping and having ice creams and eat this huge dinner and all this kind, and I'm complaining for "We're having rice every day, waaah," and they haven't got food every day.

So I really felt like I'm not appreciating the things I get, and it has affected me because I never seen this before, and I think it will in the future, because I think I will remember this for my whole life, and I'll teach my children to appreciate what they get and like that.

It is extraordinary to listen to Mai-Bente because she is so self-confident and sincere. She is stating facts and reacting to them as she states them. There is no artificiality about her, no eagerness to please. She arrived at Rio intending to talk about nuclear power, but when she saw the favelas she changed her mind. As the other speaker on nuclear power was Alina from near Chernobyl she felt she could safely leave that issue to her.

Mai-Bente was fourteen, and she still saw the issue as one of other people's welfare. These were people who lived thousands of miles from her home, but she still chose to speak of their problems rather than something specific to Norway that was also important to her. This is part of what she said at the hearing:

> In the last few days I have seen a lot which really has frightened me. I have seen and talked to street children. Every day they are suffering from hunger so they steal in order to eat. They have no home, no food, no education, no one to give them love. When they die they are forgotten ... I know you have to see it before it can make an impression on you. I have seen it, I have felt it, I have smelled it. Do something with this problem. Do something with this poverty.

I am afraid that few adults react to the evidence in this way. They step back from the sight and the smell and lose themselves in jungles of words. There is a striking example of this in the contrast between the first sentence of the United Nations Convention on the Rights of the Child and the first sentence of the Children's Appeal at Rio. (Part of one and the whole of the other appear in Appendix One.)

Overview

The Exeter University Conference on the Rights of the Child, where I first heard Mai-Bente, made me think not only about children's rights, but about human rights in general. The issues that concern children concern us all. I was reminded of my feeling that progressive schools do not just try to solve parochial problems to do with education, they investigate the moral basis of all behaviour.

When Dartington Hall School was closed I edited a book of reminiscences by ex-pupils. This was the reaction of my daughter, who had been at the school:

> The sad thing [about reading the book] was that it reminded me of how devastated I felt when trouble first hit, when I realised that just knowing that, at least somewhere, there was a group of people living together and being nice to each other and doing things for the right reasons had been a source of strength to me two hundred miles away in London.

St. John Gould, another pupil, who stayed on to finish his sixth-form education in the school's last year of existence before going on to university, wrote this for the book:

> I know that I am indebted to the school for more than my education, because they enabled me to develop my personality, free from the restraints of society, government and family. ... My history teacher, Sean, noted that whereas with places like Cambridge the atmosphere is largely based on the buildings, the atmosphere here is created by people. This is the key to understanding Dartington Hall School, particularly Aller Park [for children up to thirteen]. The atmosphere can never be recreated, for it is one based on love. Though there are mistakes made, people still act out of love.

Most adults have given up trying to do things for the right reasons, and trying to act out of love. All that involves too much thought and decision-making. It is far easier to accept one of the reach-me-down patterns from Received Ideas, the shop that peddles religions, prejudices, ethical systems and philosophies. They are generally thought to be much better than the home-made ones, and it saves so much time.

Most schools buy ready-made too, but at schools like Dartington or Sands the children make their own, "free from the restraints of society, government and family," as St. John Gould says. The answers that they find are based on concern for everybody's welfare, and they are often not the answers that would be found by following conventional social codes; they are generally far more ethical. This is not the result of prolonged philosophical discussion, it is a result of the children allowing their own natural benevolence to express itself in action. They are the kind of answers that any children would find if they were only given the opportunity.

One of the things that disturbs many adults about the sort of moral system that emerges from this freedom is the absence of a list of virtues. There is no automatic place for justice, honesty, sobriety, obedience, industry, perseverance, chastity, modesty, or courtesy. All these are subjected to the single overwhelming need to make sure that everyone is all right. This is a consequence of the nature of the world, a consequence of evolution, a requirement of the 'selfish' gene.

It was all summed up pretty well about two thousand years ago in that remark that Margaret Thatcher found it impossible to understand – "Love thy neighbour as thyself." I like to think of this not as a command but as a granting of permission. "Go on, it's all right. Don't be embarrassed by your own goodness." It does not make sense to order you to love someone, because you cannot love someone to order; on the other hand you can be grateful for approval when secretly you love someone to whom society as a whole expects you to be indifferent.

CHAPTER FOURTEEN

HEAVY AS FROST

Full soon thy soul shall have her earthly freight,
And custom lie upon thee with a weight
Heavy as frost, and deep almost as life.

William Wordsworth

One Psychologist's View

A child's morality springs from concern for other people. Lawrence Blum calls this "altruistic emotion", and considers it the proper root of all moral behaviour, and yet until recently psychologists have tried hard to demonstrate that moral understanding only develops with age. "Love thy neighbour as thyself," said Christ, and yet Christian society has shown extraordinary determination in its efforts to destroy children's confidence in their own wish to do so. Our society seems to have been actually afraid of children and to have gone out of its way to discourage and discredit them.

John Shotter is a respected psychologist who moved away from some of the old assumptions. "We must begin," he says, "by taking the same common-sense view that mothers take of their infants at birth, that they begin life in some sense as persons – albeit as very primitive ones." (*Social Accountability and Selfhood*) This view, he confirms, is by no means universal amongst psychologists, and he gives examples of earlier opinions. "Many assume that the child at first is 'asocial' (Schaffer, 1971), 'animal matter' (M. P. M. Richards, 1974), developing only as an aspect of 'embryogenesis' (Piaget and Inhalder, 1969) into a person later."

Shotter had obviously moved forward a long way. Nevertheless, his views of adulthood remain extraordinary, and some discussion of them will illuminate the perversity of many current attitudes to children.

People do not become adults, Shotter says, until they have "qualified to be treated as autonomous persons." A child, though a person, is not, in John Shotter's opinion, autonomous. "...to be autonomous, not reliant like a child upon others to complete and give the appropriate meaning to one's acts, is to be accorded the right of expressing oneself, of telling one's thoughts, feelings and intentions, and the right to be accorded their author and to be taken as responsible for them." He also says that people show maturity "by becoming responsible adults not reliant upon others to judge and evaluate their behaviour."

It is, apparently, societies that turn children into adults.

> All societies must incorporate in the operational procedures of their
> daily life, devices, 'mechanisms', social practices to do with
> 'manufacturing' from their newborns the basic elements capable of
> maintaining their social order, i.e. persons. To the extent that a society
> remains in existence, these procedures must exist somewhere (non-
> locatable) in its ecology...

In spite of allowing that children are people, Shotter is still trying to justify society's disdain for childhood. A discussion of his argument will lead me comfortably to the question of what really distinguishes an adult from a child.

According to Shotter, as a child you are not autonomous because you rely on others to evaluate your behaviour. Society works on you with various mechanisms until it has turned you into a responsible person. You can then be taken seriously at last, and become incorporated into society, thus ensuring that it remains in existence.

This is like the selfish gene theory in reverse. Dawkins says we must be selfish because genes need to survive, and they are part of us. Shotter says we must conform because society needs to survive, and we are part of it. Dawkins, as I have shown, failed to understand that one of the implications of his own theory is that humans must have a gene which makes them want to look after each other. Shotter makes the error of thinking that individuals exist for society, and not society for individuals.

Shotter says children have to acquire the ability to maintain the social order if they are to become people. It seems to me that it is at precisely the moment that children decide to maintain the social order rather than to follow their personal convictions that they stop being people and become automata.

When you are a child, Shotter says, you are reliant upon others to complete and give the appropriate meaning to your acts. I cannot make any sense of this. When I was very small I sniffed at a daisy so enthusiastically that it disappeared up my nostril and I had to be taken to the doctor. As far as I can make out I was not reliant on anybody to complete or give meaning to my act. On another occasion my mother let me have a puff at a cigarette. Unfortunately when she said "puff" I thought she meant "blow", and I blew the lighted cigarette into the pocket of her cardigan. Shotter must be referring to some other sort of act. In both cases I made mistakes, but I knew what I was trying to do – I was trying to find out what a daisy smelt like, and what it was like to smoke a cigarette. I didn't need anyone else to tell me that I hadn't got it quite right.

The idea that children need adults to evaluate their behaviour seems to have been invented entirely by adults. The adults may think so, but to the children their own actions are perfectly coherent, and adult intervention is often irrelevant and foolish.

Shotter also denies children the right to be taken as responsible for their thoughts, feelings and intentions. He must have sat in an office and thought it up; with real live children around him he couldn't have come to that conclusion. Once again he has got things exactly the wrong way round; it is his social adults who have abandoned responsibility for their thoughts, feelings and intentions by accepting the values of society.

What is an Adult?

Luckily in our civilisation it is not essential for people to abandon their consciences entirely to the safe-keeping of society, so they do preserve some independence. Part of this preservation of independence is due to the vagueness of our definition of adulthood.

There is no moment which corresponds to the initiation in a primitive tribe, where privileges and responsibilities are accorded in a single ceremony. In 1993 *Education Guardian* published a list of the rights and duties of young people, and the various ages at which they are acquired. There were forty separate items, spread between the ages of five and twenty-one. A Norwegian pamphlet with the same kind of information listed thirty-three rights and duties, two of them starting at the age of seven, and the rest spread fairly evenly between twelve and eighteen. Other western countries have similar systems, but no two systems are the same. From a legal point of view you become grown up in different ways at different ages in different countries; there is no simple definition.

The common sense idea of a grown-up is someone who has stopped growing taller. Another purely physical definition is that an adult is a person capable of sexual reproduction. The United Nations Convention on the Rights of the Child defines an adult as anyone over the age of eighteen, unless the laws of the country recognise an earlier age of majority.

The legal rights and responsibilities of an adult differ from country to country, but here are some examples from Britain. An adult is someone who does not have to go to school. An adult is financially independent. An adult is allowed to drink in a pub. An adult can gamble. An adult can sign a hire-purchase agreement. An adult is allowed to vote in elections. An adult can be sent to prison. An adult can join the army. Adults are not the legal responsibility of their parents.

Such disparate ideas imply differences between adults and children that reach beyond the physical conditions of height and sexual maturity. These are some of the implied assumptions:

All adults are wiser than children.
Adults are able to look after themselves, but children are not.
Adults are expected to contribute to society, but children are not.
Adults are trustworthy, but children are not.

Adults have a right to decide how they will spend their time and money, but children do not.

At some time which depends on the country they live in, but generally comes between the ages of twelve and eighteen, children are supposed to convert into adults. At last they are able to look after themselves, they are expected to contribute to society, they become experienced and trustworthy and they acquire a right to decide what they will do.

Some of the changes associated with adulthood happen suddenly, such as the onset of menstruation or the breaking voice, leaving school or the crucial birthday, but others are spread over years, and some over a lifetime. The picture of childhood as a gradual ascent towards a plateau of maturity is probably only applicable to physical height. Height is such a conspicuous characteristic that there is a tendency to feel that other more abstract characteristics, such as intelligence and responsibility, must behave in the same way. This does not follow. These characteristics may mature in a year or two like sexuality, or continue to grow like experience, or decline like fluid intelligence, or fluctuate like weight.

Independence from parental support is thought of as a mark of adulthood, yet in some situations people have to look after themselves and each other when they are very young. Many of the street children in South America, Africa and the East are well under the age of ten, and yet many of them manage to survive. Only adults are thought to be capable of contributing to society, but in Victorian England some people were expected to start work by the age of four, because in some jobs, such as chimney-sweeping or coal mining, it was an advantage to be small. It is reported that there are four-year-olds working in coal mines in Colombia today.

The boundaries of adulthood are extremely difficult to define.

The Need For A Statement Of Children's Rights

The Convention on the Rights of the Child, as adopted by the United Nations in 1989, is another indication of the limited areas in which you can distinguish clearly between adults and children. There are forty-one articles, which take up eleven pages; this is a summary of some of the most important rights:

The right to life.

The right to adequate food, water, clothes and dwelling-place.

The right to health care.

The right to education.

The right to live with your parents, or, if this is impossible, with people who will care for you.

The right to follow your own religion and enjoy your own culture.

The right to a name and a nationality.

The right to be protected from any form of exploitation, including sale into adoption, sexual abuse, child labour and enrolment in the armed forces.

The right to express opinions and have them taken into account.

The right to information.

The right to privacy.

A disabled child's right to special care, education and training.

Almost all these rights are listed in the 1948 United Nations Universal Declaration of Human Rights. The obvious exception is the right to live with your parents. There are also some special rights in relation to adoption and the administration of justice. If children were considered to be automatically entitled to all human rights, these are the only children's rights that would have had to be specified. The reason we have to have a Convention on the Rights of the Child is not that children have different needs from adults, but that they are not considered to be fully human, and that their basic human rights are therefore often ignored.

KinderRÄchTsZÄnke, the Berlin children's group founded in 1992 to fight for children's rights, is only asking for equality, not for anything more. It asks that children should have the same rights as adults. The idea is still seen as revolutionary today (in 2010).

Children see Themselves as Inferior

The KinderRÄchTsZÄnker publish a poster which consists entirely of typical adult remarks to children. A rough translation begins like this:

What is that supposed to be. Go away. You won't get a second helping. Stop jabbering. Say sorry. Why aren't you doing anything. You're too little. Where did you find that. Good boy. Be quiet. Sit up straight. Don't you talk to your parents like that. Behave yourself. Leave it alone. Don't be such a cry-baby. I've already told you a hundred times. Say thank you. It's out of the question. Where were you this time. You ought to be ashamed. If you had a glimmer of understanding. Don't make a face like that. There's no need to be afraid. Haven't you got ears. You eat what's on the table. You've made a nice mess of that. You don't say that. If I catch you again. Do you always have to have the last word. Stop it.

And that is only about a quarter of it.

Small children often have almost everything decided for them – what they wear, what they eat, where they sit, who they play with. Their opinions are not even consulted, let alone taken seriously. Children are often used to being laughed at, slapped, shouted at, openly criticised, manhandled and publicly undressed without the attendant adult being aware that there might be any cause of embarrassment or humiliation. Children are taught that they are insignificant, and if they accept this view, then obviously nothing that they do can matter much. The only way they can draw attention to themselves is by doing something that successfully disturbs or annoys the adults round them. Probably the child who misbehaves in these circumstances is healthier than the one who remains in an acquiescent coma, but there is little to be achieved by it. If the adults are not interested in you, you have no satisfactory way of influencing their behaviour. They can do what they like, and they have no need to take your feelings into account.

This perception of childhood as an inferior status persists. At the World Conference on the Rights of the Child at Exeter University in 1992 there was a panel of 20 young people who assessed the proceedings and reported back to the plenary session at the end of each day. Their ages ranged from 13 to 18, and they objected to being referred to as children.

They were therefore called "young people", which was perhaps a necessary change; it was important that their contributions to the conference should be taken seriously, and even at a conference on the rights of the child there were people who found it difficult to treat children with respect. The young people themselves thought only about two-thirds of the adults managed it. I would have liked them to have been proud of being children; they were accorded extra importance at the conference precisely because they were children, and yet they were often put down, and felt more respected if they could drop the label 'child'.

A View from Dickens

The effectiveness of the disrespect which adults show to children was recognised by Charles Dickens. He wrote a story called *Mrs. Orange* which illustrated it. In this story the children are in charge and the people who are ordered about, condescended to, patronised and referred to as "children" are actually the grown-ups. Perhaps a few quotations will throw light on John Shotter's notion of children's actions needing adults to give them meaning.

This is what happens when Mrs. Orange visits Mrs. Lemon's school.

Mrs. Lemon took Mrs. Orange into the schoolroom where there were a number of pupils. "Stand up, children," said Mrs. Lemon; and they all stood up.

Mrs. Orange whispered to Mrs. Lemon, "There is a pale, bald child, with red whiskers, in disgrace. Might I ask what he has done?"

"Come here, White," said Mrs. Lemon, "and tell this lady what you have been doing."

"Betting on horses," said White, sulkily.

"Are you sorry for it, you naughty child?" said Mrs. Lemon.

"No," said White. "Sorry to lose, but shouldn't be sorry to win."

"There's a vicious boy for you, ma'am," said Mrs. Lemon. "Go along with you, sir. This is Brown, Mrs. Orange. Oh, a sad case, Brown's! Never knows when he has had enough. Greedy. How is your gout, sir?"

"Bad!" said Brown.

"What else can you expect?" said Mrs. Lemon. "Your stomach is the size of two. Go and take exercise directly. Mrs. Black, come here to me. Now, here is a child, Mrs. Orange, ma'am, who is always at play. She can't be kept at home a single day together; always gadding about and spoiling her clothes. Play, play, play, play, from morning to night and to morning again. How can she expect to improve?"

"Don't expect to improve!" sulked Mrs. Black. "Don't want to."

Today children are still expected to confess their mistakes to strangers, they are still publicly rebuked for their appetites, still exhorted to take exercise when they don't want to, still required to stay at home instead of playing with their friends. The fact that adults are treated differently is certainly not due to the fact that they behave any better.

These are a few incidents from Mrs. Alicumpaine's children's party.

"My dear James," cried Mrs. Orange, who had been peeping about, "do look here. Here's the supper for the darlings, ready laid in the room, behind the folding-doors.

"Here's their little pickled salmon, I do declare! And here's their little salad, and their little roast beef and fowls, and their little pastry, and their wee, wee, wee champagne!"

It may seem heavy-handed to comment on the point of satire, but I have to draw attention to the way that Dickens has shown that to be different is not necessarily to be ridiculous.

Four tiresome fat boys would stand in the doorway and talk about the newspapers, until Mrs. Alicumpaine went to them and said, "My dears, I really cannot allow you to prevent people from coming in. I shall be truly sorry to do it; but if you put yourself in everybody's way I must positively send you home."

You cannot really send adults home, but you can send children home perfectly easily. You are under no obligation to show children even the most basic courtesy.

"What are they doing now?" said Mrs. Orange to Mrs. Alicumpaine.

"They are making speeches and playing at Parliament," said Mrs. Alicumpaine to Mrs. Orange.

On hearing this, Mrs. Orange set off once more back again to Mr. Orange, and said, "James, dear, do come. The children are playing at Parliament."

"Thank you, my dear," said Mr. Orange, "but I don't care about Parliament, myself."

So Mrs. Orange went once again without Mr. Orange to the room where the children were having supper to see them playing at Parliament. And she found some of the boys crying "Hear, hear, hear!" while other boys cried, "No, no!" and others "Question!" "Spoke!" and all sorts of nonsense that ever you heard.

... But at last Mrs. Alicumpaine said, "I cannot have this din. Now, children, you have played at Parliament very nicely; but Parliament gets tiresome after a little while, and it's time you left off for you will soon be fetched."

These "children" understand what they are doing, but Mrs. Orange and Mrs. Alicumpaine accord their actions no particular meaning at all. It looks as though John Shotter was right to notice that much of what children do is incomprehensible to adults. He was wrong to assume that what adults find incomprehensible is necessarily meaningless.

The Selfish Society

The things that physically distinguish an adult from a child are chronological age, sexual maturity and having reached full height. It is also observable that children grow, and are usually full of curiosity and energy. Adults deteriorate.

Physically, adults deteriorate: when they are forty they cannot run as fast as they used to be able to. Their senses deteriorate: they cannot see or hear as well as they did. In terms of fluid intelligence, they deteriorate. Their intuitive sympathy with others becomes less acute. They tend to abandon their own judgement in favour of the judgement of society. They grow only in terms of crystallised intelligence, that is to say in knowledge and in certain skills.

In order for society to survive it needs knowledgeable and skilful servants who will accept its values and pursue its interests without worrying about their individual consciences. It therefore rewards older people with power. The consequence of this is that young people's idealistic visions of change are disregarded, and the selfish society maintains its identity.

Nevertheless, the selfish society is not omnipotent. It is possible for adults to retain some of that empathy and altruism that came to them so easily as children, and to use their knowledge and skill for purposes of their own. With growing confidence in themselves, some adults learn to throw off the mask that society has obliged them to wear, and to trust in their own feelings once again.

I do not know how much of our loss of natural empathy is biologically determined, like the loss of fluid intelligence, and how much is due to the influence of society, and I do not know at what age the decline begins, but my inclination is to believe that the biological loss starts during adolescence, and the institutional influence begins at birth. The institutional influence can be corrected, but any biological change, like the menopause, is presumably irreversible.

This is not as pessimistic a view as it may appear at first sight. At whatever age our moral sensitivity starts to decline, and whatever the cause of its decline, we can still appreciate its importance as we grow older, just as we continue to appreciate athletic excellence when we ourselves can manage no more than a lumbering trot. And just as we can extend our active lives by regular exercise and by taking part in sport, so we can increase our moral awareness by deliberately exercising it.

A Shocking Suggestion

The idea of exercising our moral awareness makes us flinch. We are satisfied with our moral standards as they are; we have set limits to our own generosity and tolerance precisely because we feel those limits are reasonable and fair. We don't want to be any better than we are. We are afraid of what might happen if we deliberately exercised our better qualities and taught ourselves to rely on our natural benevolence.

The implications of this are so revolutionary that I only dare to put them in the form of questions.

- Can it be that our longstanding belief that the world is only made bearable by the fact that we control our passions with our wills is not only wrong but the exact reverse of the truth?

- Can it be that in so far as we control our passions by force of will we actually prevent ourselves from doing a great deal of good that we would otherwise be eager to do?

- Can it be that we are frightened, not that if we give way to our feelings we will become uncontrollably evil, completely subject to lust, hatred and greed, but that if we give way to our feelings we will become uncontrollably good, devoting ourselves entirely to the welfare of others?

- Is part of the process of growing up the deliberate repression of our altruistic emotion?

- Does society ensure its own survival by precisely this mechanism, because if the mechanism did not exist society would surely change?

The passage I quoted from John Shotter near the beginning of this chapter suggests that this might well be so.

All societies must incorporate in the operational procedures of their daily life, devices, 'mechanisms', social practices to do with 'manufacturing' from their newborns the basic elements capable of maintaining their social order, i.e. persons. To the extent that a society remains in existence, these procedures must exist somewhere (non-locatable) in its ecology.

Our society is plainly not perfect, so we must wish it to change for the better, yet if John Shotter is right, and in this respect I believe he is, society itself has incorporated devices for turning newborns into the basic elements that will maintain the social order. In order to survive in its present form, society has had to do its best to become self-perpetuating, regardless of the welfare of its individual members. We have been manipulated into becoming willing slaves to invisible institutions. If the world is to become a better place, we must throw off our chains.

The Adult's Responsibility

An English advisory teacher who is distressed at much of what she sees in the schools she visits, wrote this:

> I am constantly asking myself whether I should be a silent witness to the endless subtle abuse of children's integrity and glowing potential. It amazes me that anyone who has children of their own can fail to see the great capacity of children to order their own lives, motivated by a powerful drive to learn ... about everything.

Children have integrity and glowing potential, but they have no power. Adults have power and experience, but they have no independence. Power and experience are tools, not virtues. As we get older we acquire better and better equipment, but we use it in the service of the wrong masters. We have been trained to forget what we should use it for. Our children have not yet forgotten.

Adults have the power to make changes in our society, but they have learnt to fear change. They want to retain the status quo for fear of something worse. Children understand that the status quo must be changed, if we are ever to attain anything better. It is the adults who will have to make the changes, but before they can do so they will have to learn to listen.

Carol Gilligan Again

Carol Gilligan tells us that men are usually primarily concerned with a justice ethic, and women are usually primarily concerned with an ethic of caring. As a psychologist she analyses what is, she does not suggest what ought to be. As a woman she cannot simply say that the predominantly male approach is wrong, because she would then be open to charges of irrational sexism and an inability to understand the superior male standpoint. I am not a psychologist, and I am a man. I can therefore assert:

(1)   that the justice approach is at best a secondary consideration and is often quite simply wrong, and

(2)   that the caring approach is the basis of all true morality.

Justice, as David Hume said in the 18th century, is an artificial virtue. "'Tis only from selfishness and confin'd generosity of men, along with the scanty provision nature has made for his wants, that justice derives its origin," he wrote, and "If men pursu'd the publick interest naturally, and with a hearty affection, they wou'd never have dream'd of restraining each other by these rules." This is a case in which the word 'men' should not be thought to imply 'men and women', because women are likely to be less selfish and more generous than men, and to pursue the public interest naturally with a hearty affection. As far as women are concerned, justice is not only an artificial virtue, it is also an unnecessary one.

Gilligan takes for granted the fact that adolescents are deeply involved in moral questions. In the following quotation, unusually, she does not even feel the need to quote research to confirm what she says.

> In the life cycle the adolescent is the truth teller, like the fool in the Renaissance play, exposing hypocrisy and revealing truths about human relationships. These truths pertain to justice and care, the moral coordinates of human connection, heightened for adolescents who stand between the innocence of childhood and the responsibility of adulthood. Looking back on the childhood experiences of inequality and attachment, feeling again the powerlessness and vulnerability which these experiences initially evoked, adolescents identify with the child and construct a world that offers protection. This ideal or utopian vision, laid out along the coordinates of justice and care, depicts a world where self and other will be treated as of equal worth, where, despite differences in power, things will be fair; a world where everyone will be included, where no one will be left alone or hurt. – *Exit-Voice Dilemmas in Adolescent Development* in *Mapping the Moral Domain*

Carol Gilligan understands the adolescent's idealism, but she is cautious about expounding its implications. Psychologists are scientists who observe, record and analyse behaviour; they are not supposed to become emotionally involved. Nevertheless, she allows herself to go thus far:

> As the contemporary reality of global interdependence impels the
> search for new maps of development, the exploration of attachment
> may provide the psychological grounding for new visions of progress
> and growth.

Let me put it more bluntly. The justice ethic has no answer to poverty, war or the threat of environmental disaster; our only hope is to adopt an ethic of care. The important thing is not to make rules and punish those who break them, but simply to ensure that, as far as possible, everyone is all right.

CHAPTER FIFTEEN

ALLOWING CHILDREN TO DIRECT
THEIR OWN LIVES

Prenez garde à ce petit être;
Il est bien grand, il contient dieu.

Victor Hugo

Just after my first book, *Considering Children*, had been published, I was interviewed by someone who said it was all very well to say that adolescents should be allowed to direct their own lives, but at what age did I think this self-direction should start. At the time I had no answer. I had not yet read anything by Penelope Leach or Alison Stallibrass.

The Very Beginning

When young parents want to find out how to look after their babies or small children a book they may well refer to is *Baby and Child*, by Penelope Leach. It is full of practical advice on feeding, sleep, health and hygiene, but it is different from its predecessors in an extremely important way. It invites the parents to consider all these things from the baby's point of view.

It is not long ago that this approach would have been considered absurd. A baby was just a bundle of reflexes. It was not thought possible for a baby to have a point of view. What mattered was keeping the baby clean and warm and fed with as little trouble to the parents as possible. A newborn baby had no experience, knew nothing and could be easily trained to be docile and undemanding if the right approach was used from the very beginning. Only sentimental parents endowed their babies with personalities; realistic parents were expected to be able to do their duty by their children without any such fantasy.

At what point is it reasonable to start thinking about the child's point of view? This is Penelope Leach's answer.

Brutally forced through a tight passage from a soft, quiet, warm, dark haven into a world of light and noise and texture, every bit of the baby's nervous system reacts with shock. But his struggles are not over. The placenta which fed his circulation oxygen from your bloodstream, has finished its work. He must breathe. His lungs have never expanded before. The effort of that first breath must be fearful. But if he can make it alone, we need not add the pain of a slapped bottom. We are so used to slapping newborns and hearing their first cry that we have almost forgotten that there can be breath without crying.

If he is to breathe easily, his nose and mouth must be clear of amniotic fluid and mucus. But if he can clear them himself, we need not torment him with tubes. We are so used to routine suction for new babies that we have forgotten how those tubes must feel to him.

Safely breathing, the baby needs time to rest and to discover that even though the womb has ejected him, there is still comfort in his world. Your belly, soft and slack now, forms an ideal cradle. On it, he can be almost as comfortable as he was in it. There he can rest.

But he cannot rest unless his surroundings are toned down. The midwives needed those glaring lights for a safe delivery, but he is safely delivered now. Turn them down. They hurt the baby's eyes. He has never seen light before.

The midwives needed to talk and to move around during the delivery. But there is nothing now that cannot wait. Be quiet. Your noises frighten him. All sounds have been muffled for him until now.

If all is dim and quiet, warm and peaceful, the baby will relax after his traumatic journey. His breathing will steady. His crumpled face will smooth itself out and his eyes will open. His head will lift a little and his limbs will move against your skin. Put very gently to your bare breast, he may suck, discover a new form of human contact and feel a little less separated. These are his first contacts with his new world: let him make them without distress. These are his first moments of life; let him have them in peace.

And so the book goes on. It has all the necessary medical information and advice on feeding and sleeping problems, but the child is always taken seriously as a person with the same rights as anyone else. This is not a way-out, progressive approach to babies, it is a standard text-book for parents.

Penelope Leach tells the mother that "your baby will learn to love you with a determined and unshakeable passion unequalled in human relationships." This is very different from the old view that a child's emotions are short-lived and therefore unimportant.

The Playgroup
Alison Stallibrass's book *The Self-Respecting Child*, first published in 1974, is about the way a free-choice playgroup can help children to develop. When she says "free-choice" she means exactly what she says.

The children's choice must be absolutely spontaneous and uninfluenced by any ulterior motives such as pleasing mother or teacher or escaping from boredom: a "don't mind if I do" attitude on their part is not good enough, neither is asking them to choose between two alternatives of our choosing. They must feel free to do nothing if that is what they prefer, and they must feel that what they are able to choose to do is what they want to do more than anything else at the moment. They must be able to respond directly and quite unselfconsciously to the environment. If there is an adult supervising the children's play who has a preconceived idea of what the children should be doing, or guides them and directs them in any way, however gently, little will be discovered.

But when children are allowed this freedom, they discover a great deal. Because it happens so naturally and with no adult intervention, visiting adults may find it difficult to observe. In this passage Alison Stallibrass emphasises what unsympathetic visitors may miss by describing what they may see.

The casual visitor to the playgroup may not easily become aware of the "amiable circle" of development that is in operation before his eyes, each child adding his individual and original contribution to the environment and also taking from the environment created by all, the particular educational nourishment he needs. He may not even notice the dynamic order that prevails, apparently in spite of, but in reality *because of* the real freedom and spontaneity of the children.

This dynamic harmony is a physical one as well as a social one, and it is most clearly observed in physical terms. One of the essential conditions is that there should be no adult interference.

... some adults think that spontaneity of movement exercised by a large group of children in a comparatively small and encumbered space must be dangerous. But small children are alive to the messages being sent out constantly by all their senses; and if they are in an atmosphere where there is nothing to be gained by "showing off", and where they know they are responsible for themselves, there will be few bumps and bruises. It has been shown that, when children are digesting the knowledge of how to climb, jump, slide, swing and run, together with and among, and in and out and around about others, they manifest what – in the case of the children in the Peckham Health Centre gymnasium – was described by Scott Williamson as "physical altruism."

I like the term "physical altruism", which suggests an identification with the needs of others in an absolutely literal sense. The concern which children show for each other when playing is also demonstrated by the fact that a great deal of what they do when they play by themselves without adult organisers involves complex skills but no competition – for instance hopscotch, jacks, skipping and skateboarding. There may be an effort to outdo someone else, but this does not entail doing the other person down.

When I met Alison Stallibrass I told her of my inability to answer when I was asked how old children should be before being allowed to make their own decisions about their lives. She told me that her dilemma, though similar, was the reverse: she had a problem when she was asked how long you should go on allowing children to make their own decisions.

My book, *Considering Children*, with its subtitle "A parents' guide to progressive education", was outside the mainstream of educational thinking, but *The Self-Respecting Child* was for a while widely accepted as the proper guide to pre-school education. It has been published as a Penguin Education Special and as part of Addison-Wesley's series *Classics in Child Development*. To my surprise I realised that in some respects young children are generally regarded as more able to look after themselves than those who are old enough to go to school.

The Peckham Health Centre

For children of school age, having the chance of being treated as responsible people has depended on where they lived. If you were fourteen at the beginning of the '70s and lived near Countesthorpe in Leicestershire you were lucky, if you lived in Islington in the early '60s you might have gone to Risinghill, but one of the best times and places to be a child in Britain seems to have been Peckham between 1935 and 1939.

The importance of the Peckham Experiment is enormous, and yet in spite of its success it is surprisingly little known. My source of information is *Being me and also us*, also by Alison Stallibrass. She worked at the health centre as a student-assistant, and it was there that she learnt many of the principles that she put into practice in her free-choice play-group. The book is a blend of research and personal observations, and provides ample evidence to confirm the impression she describes in her prologue: "I felt that I was assisting in an enterprise that offered the best chance there was of changing the world for the better." It is extraordinary that the health centre has not been widely imitated.

It was founded under the direction of two doctors, George Williamson and Innes Pearse, and was not a health centre in the modern sense, a place that deals with people who are not healthy, but a centre that was to promote health and happiness. They chose Peckham because they wanted an area that was not too wealthy, on the one hand, but was not handicapped by extreme poverty on the other. Most of the wage-earners were tradesmen, small business-men, clerical workers or steadily employed artisans. The centre itself was a large modern building of three floors containing a swim-ming-pool, a theatre, a gymnasium, a recreation area with billiards tables, table-tennis tables and dart-boards, a cafeteria, several large adaptable spaces that could be used for ball-room dancing, band practice, meetings and social occasions, and the doctors' consulting rooms, which took up less than a quarter of the top floor.

Alison Stallibrass quotes from Williamson and Pearse's report of the first eighteen months of the centre:

Our failures during our first eighteen months' work have taught us something very significant. Individuals, from infants to old people, resent or fail to show any interest in anything initially presented to them through discipline, regulation or instruction which is another aspect of authority.

... Having provided the members with a chance to do things, we find that we have to leave them to make their own use of them. We have had to learn to sit back and wait for these activities to emerge. Any impatience on our part, translated into help, has strangled their efforts – we have had to cultivate more and more patience in ourselves. The alternative to this cultivation of patience is, of course, obvious – the application of compulsion in one or other of its many forms, perhaps the most tempting of which is persuasion. But having a fundamental interest in the source and origin of spontaneous action –

as all biologists must – we have had to discard even that instrument for initiating activities.

This approach was applied to all individuals, from infants to old people. From the beginning, crowds of children invaded the Centre every day after school was over. They found they could go where they liked, except for the gym and the swimming pool, where they were only allowed in if they were supervised. They ran wild, racing up and down the stairs and the halls, and using the heavy glass ashtrays for games of curling on the polished cork floors. Adult users of the Centre complained, but Williamson and Pearce insisted that to control the children's behaviour by authority would be to remove their opportunity of learning responsibility.

The problem was solved by the appointment of Lucy Crocker. First she asked the children what they wanted to do – they wanted to learn to swim, they would love to have gym classes and so on. She created a careful timetable with the children's co-operation, and the scheme was launched. Hardly anyone turned up. It seemed that, if use of the swimming pool and the gymnasium meant attending regular classes and submitting to the control of an instructor, they would rather do without it.

The alternative was to allow the children to use the facilities as individually as the adults did. Lucy Crocker devised a method that enabled each child to choose spontaneously what to do from moment to moment. All they had to do was get permission, in the form of a ticket signed by herself or a deputy. This ticket would admit the child to the pool or gymnasium, or allow use of one of the adult recreation facilities, and served as a check on the borrowing of the roller-skates, scooters, small bicycles, jigsaws, art and craft materials and board games that were also available.

There was no regular supervision in the pool or in the gym, in spite of the apparent danger of the ropes and wall-bars, beams and vaulting bucks. Through giving out the tickets Lucy knew roughly who was where, and she could walk around the open-plan first floor and see into the centrally situated swimming pool and down into the gym and badminton court through the part glass dividing walls. The children quickly became aware that they were responsible for their own safety and enjoyment, and behaved accordingly. In four and a half years there was only one serious accident – a broken arm; this record compares favourably with what might have been expected to happen in organised gym classes.

Within a short time from the introduction of this system, the attitude of the children in the Centre, and the attitude of the adults towards the children, had both been transformed.

Visitors to the Centre began to remark on the purposeful air of the children as they moved around the building, on their serenity and poise and the direct and friendly way in which they responded to a stranger's questions.

The purpose of a child at the Centre was usually to learn skills one at a time. Weeks of playing in the gym, learning to swing and balance, jump and climb, would be followed by weeks in the pool, finding out all the different ways of moving through water, and later experimenting with moving through air while jumping in. There was no place in their activities for competition or performance; they developed skills for their own sake.

A short example of this learning style is given in some of Alison Stallibrass's own notes:

Brian O [aged just four] was away from school owing to a cold – asked for skates, insisted on keeping them on for three hours. The next day he had them on for 4 hours and the same every day for a week. By the end of the week he could skate fast and well and turn corners with skill.

Brian was a bit anti-social in the nursery and uncontrolled in his behaviour. Now that he goes to school, comes to the Centre on his own and goes when and where he likes, he is a responsible person. No-one bothers about him and he bothers no-one else. There was a very short period at first when he was up to mischief.

The temptation to quote more is strong, but anyone who is interested can read the book for themselves. I will limit myself to one more paragraph which shows that the children's social development moved as smoothly as their physical skills.

At the Centre no instance of bullying was ever observed by any member of staff. There appeared also to be no 'daring' of each other by the children during their play. I can think of three possible reasons for this absence of aggressive power seeking. Firstly, they had no need to repel boredom by teasing, competing, fighting, establishing dominance or other potentially anti-social and dangerous activities. Secondly, each child was aware that he, together with the other children, was responsible for the preservation of the play-situation that he valued so highly; and thirdly, having acquired considerable power over themselves and over physical forces and things, they had little desire for power over other people, and felt no compulsion to boost their self-esteem by obtaining it.

The experiment was brought to an end by outbreak of the war with Germany, but four and a half years had been long enough to demonstrate, among many other things, that ordinary children know what is good for them, both physically and socially. As long as the right opportunities are available they will take what they need with restraint and responsibility.

CHAPTER SIXTEEN

AND AT SCHOOL, TOO

Children also know what is good for them at school. This has also been demonstrated in many experimental schools around the world. It is not only in their social life that children benefit from freedom to decide for themselves. It is also in their learning.

Most present-day adults in the West will remember being forced to waste an enormous amount of their time in school. Even though, some of the time, we were interested and involved, we spent hours waiting for teachers to arrive, waiting for them to establish order in the classroom, listening to other children making mistakes, being too afraid to ask questions when we didn't understand, sitting at desks while teachers talked about subjects that meant nothing to us, spending much effort learning information that, had it been relevant to us, we could have learnt in a single reading, mindlessly writing out other people's opinions or copying information from the people sitting next to us. By the time we were sixteen the cleverest and most biddable among us had collected enough skills and information to pass a respectable number of exams, and by the time we were twenty we had forgotten most of what we had learnt. Some of us were even instructed to forget it; I have several times heard of university lecturers telling their students to forget what they had learned at school because now they were going to learn something completely different.

There have been, and there are, schools where the pattern of learning is not like this. At the Fundación Educativa Pestalozzi in Ecuador, for example, the staff provide learning materials, but they do nothing to persuade the children to use them. They believe that unless children learn to make choices for themselves early in life, they will never learn to make sensible choices as they get older. It was founded in 1977, and has been a proven success. At the Democratic School of Hadera, in Israel, there is a huge range of courses and opportunities, but no one is obliged to go to any of them. At the Butterflies organisation for street and working children in Delhi, the children who come have to be so determined to learn that they are prepared to give up valuable working time, during which they might otherwise earn a little money for food and clothes. They come in their hundreds. At Sudbury Valley School in Massachusetts there are no lessons; children spend their days as they wish, and learn what they want to learn. Sudbury Valley has the whole of the next chapter to itself.

These are extreme examples of places where children learn without pressure being put upon them, and they are far afield. However, there is no need for us inhibited Britons to look abroad. Clear evidence of the success of self-determined learning can be found within the state system in this country. I will give four widely differing examples, in chronological order.

Prestolee Elementary School, 1918 – 1951
Prestolee Elementary School, in a Lancashire working-class area, surrounded by mills and a power-station, was run for thirty-three years by E. F. O'Neill.

O'Neill believed that teachers should do things with children rather than for them, that children should be allowed to choose their own activities and follow them through for as long as they wished, that a fixed timetable destroyed initiative and hampered persistence, that the ability to find out was more important than information learned by heart, that children should have the opportunity to learn from one another and that the function of a teacher was "to release the life force which is latent in ever child; to provide opportunities for it to exercise and to facilitate such exercise in every possible way and never withhold opportunities." (Gerard Holmes, in *The Idiot Teacher*, his book about Prestolee and O'Neill.)

Edmond Holmes, once a chief inspector of schools, was an enthusiastic supporter. In the school's first year he wrote a report which included the following:

Mr. O'Neill has had effective charge of his new school for only eight months. What he has accomplished in those few months borders on the miraculous. If the school, before he took charge of it, was, as no doubt it was, of the orthodox conventional type, then I can say, without exaggeration, that an entirely new school has come into being. And if I were to characterize in a few words the change that has been effected I would say that learning by doing has taken the place of learning by swallowing.

No one in England knows better than I do what learning by swallowing means. I inspected elementary schools for nearly six years and during the whole of that time learning by doing was the very rare exception and learning by swallowing was the almost universal rule. For the first half of my inspectorial career, learning by swallowing was compulsory, and it was my duty as an Inspector – a duty which I discharged with much zeal and diligence – to see that it was systematically carried out. The children sat in blocks called classes, and opened their mouths like so many fledgelings at the word of command, and the teacher then dropped into their mouths pellets of information – rules, definitions, names, dates, tables, formulae, and the like. These pellets of information were as a rule either semi-digested or indigestible, the result being that the young fledgelings who had swallowed them made poor growth and seldom found their wings. The child who is learning by swallowing is at best learning the one thing he is required to learn: and he is learning nothing else, or very little else. His memory is perhaps being hypertrophied, but the rest of his faculties are being atrophied, starved for want of exercise.

But the child who is learning by doing is learning many things besides the one thing he is supposed to be learning. He is learning to desire, to purpose, to place, to initiate, to execute: he is learning to profit by experience, to think, to reason, to judge. And he is learning one other thing: he is learning to co-operate with others, to work for a common end, to feel the glow of comradeship.

The result was a school overflowing with activity. Every day started with a lesson about some topic of interest to the children, which was followed by a session of what were called "primaries", that is to say reading, writing and arithmetic. Children would work independently at their own pace, and some of them would have done their "primary" work at home the previous evening, in order to have more time to follow up their own interests. Others might choose to continue with their primary work for much of the rest of the day, which was to be used for whatever the children chose to do: playing, making furniture, gardening, reading, research (which might include aspects of history, geography, physics and all the rest of the traditional curriculum), talking, cooking, sewing, writing stories, painting or joining in with community singing, dancing or games.

When I say "the rest of the day" I mean more than would be meant in a normal school. There were, for instance, no set break-times. Teachers and children ate and rested when they wanted to. And after 1924 the school re-opened in the evenings and children were able to return to carry on with the activities that had been engrossing them during the day. Not only present pupils returned; some who had left school and were already at work would come too. And then parents turned up to fetch their children home and found themselves enjoying the company, helping with the preparation of snacks and drinks and staying for the whole evening. The school became a community centre.

I have seen a scrap of film of the school which was shown on television some years ago, and I was delighted and astonished by the enthusiasm and activity of the children. In his book Gerard Holmes describes the scene as a visitor might have seen it.

One comes upon a garden lounge. Children sit at it drinking their milk and by it is a brazier. In colder weather it is alight and the drinkers can warm themselves. There are flights of a few steps at either end. If you sit on the topmost, you have a new prospect. Indeed, you can see into the sand-pit. This is a low, walled enclosure, with a rather wild garden round it aglow with flag irises, dusty-miller, loganberries, crab-apples, pears, and roses; you might easily miss it and the four small people who are busy building castles in the deep sand. And you will only come upon the wishing-well by a chance turn. Its parapet is about thigh-high, and it is this parapet that really holds the water. Overhead is a roof and under this is the bucket-winding gear. The parapet was built by girls; just bricks, dipped in creamy cement, but properly bonded and brushed over internally with a cement skin and touched up here and there with the aid of a pastry knife. Boys made the wooden structure overhead, and the axle of the winding gear, an old railing, was bent to form a handle at one end by heating it in a small bonfire. The bucket is rather fun. In the bottom are rings of holes, and a disc of rubber is fitted, which acts as a valve, so that when the bucket is lowered into the water this latter, entering through the holes in the bottom and pushing past the rubber disc, fills the vessel. When it is wound up it will empty slowly through an outer ring of holes not covered by the valve, forming a shower-bath, which aerates the water in the well. This is a good thing because those are real fish which you can see swimming in the well and they like it. Children love to play with water, especially when it sprays and splashes, and there is grand exercise to be had winding the bucket up, holding it while it discharges, and lowering it to refill. The water in the well is not really deep, just eighteen inches or so, and when a child leans with his elbows on the top of the parapet, the surface is just at hand. There is a wide step at one side for smaller people to get onto. All around are roses. There are pillars of roses, trelliswork covered with climbers and ramblers, standard roses, bush roses, and pergolas where roses sprawl with other plants. That is 'Blackpool Tower ', that tall trellis structure where the girls on the ladders are tying up new shoots and pruning older growths.

And here, there, and everywhere are real fruit trees and, since the initial excitement is over, real fruit is allowed really to ripen on their branches. The longing in Teddy's [O'Neill's] mind is that every possible kind of fruit tree should be planted around and near the school, so that children should eat their fruits fresh from the branches. It is, of course, naughty to pick someone else's apples: but we may pick blackberries, and what a joy it is to do so! So walnuts, chestnuts, figs, medlars, damsons, nuts, and even peach trees and a vine, and, of course, apples, pears, plums, and a cherry were planted, one by one, in the lido; and their fruits began to supply Vitamin ED (for education). Please watch what you are treading on – that long trailing stalk with the rosette of leaves: follow it back: you see? Yes, real strawberries in a Lancashire school garden, and all over the place!

In this lido there are plants which can scratch one, and children do not like being scratched. But they do like to avoid being scratched and to dodge these prickles, and that is why there are so many deliberate obstructions and constructions – stiles, gates, ladders, and the like – in unexpected places, which one can climb over and wriggle under, avoiding these trailing thorns.

Yes, that is the windmill! Fine, isn't it? Two boys built it, complete with sails and a filter bed for that paddling-pool near by. It is as high as a house and has two balconies. The upper room is used by girls when donning their bathing-costumes, and the lower is just the place for a tea-party. It is approached by a path and surrounded by a parterre of crazy paving.

The very first boys from the village to go on to the Grammar School were, on admission, placed below what was normal for their age, as they had not been following a grammar school curriculum. They rose rapidly and soon overtook their contemporaries. One became head boy. Two of them went to university and took up teaching. One became a headmaster and the other became a Director of Education. For children from an Elementary School, at a time when only about 1% of eighteen-year-olds went to university and that 1% was almost exclusively middle-class, this was extraordinary.

And yet the Prestolee model was not imitated. Edmund Holmes, the ex-inspector, thought it necessary to advise O'Neill to "lie low. Play Brer Rabbit. Say nuffin." In spite of lying low he ran into plenty of trouble, which he survived only through the support of the parents. As far as I know, there has never been another primary school like it.

Risinghill Comprehensive School, 1960 – 1965

Risinghill was in Islington, at the time a deprived area of London. Under its headmaster, Michael Duane, it lasted only five years, but during those five years it demonstrated not only the success of a liberal approach but also two negative factors: firstly the problems arising for a while when authority is abandoned before democracy has taken root, and secondly the virulent hostility of educational authorities and the press.

Risinghill's tough, inner-city location was not its only disadvantage. A quarter of the children were immigrants, and many did not understand English adequately. The school was new, and had been formed by amalgamating two secondary modern schools and two technical schools. (At that time children were sent either to grammar schools, secondary modern schools or technical schools, on the basis of an exam taken at the age of 11.) Three of these schools had been single-sex, there was strong rivalry between them and all the heads had believed in firm discipline and control.

Soon after the school opened Duane stopped insisting on school uniform, set up a school council where the majority of members were children, kept his study door open for any child or parent to drop in without being summoned or waiting for an appointment, listened to the children's points of view when teachers complained about them, and stopped using the cane, at that time a universal feature in British schools.

For a while there was chaos, but by the end of eighteen months an orderly tradition had been established, and children who were used to the atmosphere were taking care of newcomers themselves.

Nevertheless, the government inspectors who visited the school in 1962 were not pleased. Michael Duane, they said, disapprovingly, "esteems cordiality among the major virtues," and "Sometimes in avoiding terror the school has abandoned awe."

One result of this cordiality and abandonment of awe was a rise in academic achievement. In spite of the school having only 1% of its pupils in the top fifth of the ability range, the number of candidates for the O-Level exam, intended only for that top fifth, rose from 5 in the first year to 42 in the last, and by the end of its time three children were taking the advanced level exam, and two of these went on to university – this at a time when still only a very small proportion of all school leavers did so.

Another result was a social one. When Duane started the school there were 98 children on probation. When the school was closed there were only 9.

In spite of these clearly measurable achievements, the cordiality and absence of awe and the disorder of the first year of the school were enough to justify the closure of the school, and Michael Duane, in spite of many applications, was never appointed as head of another school.

Countesthorpe College, 1976 – 1981

Countesthorpe College was founded in 1971, and it still exists, but it took five years to settle down, and its golden age only lasted another five. The pupils were between fourteen and eighteen years old, and the first two year-groups were split up into what were called "teams", each of about 100 children with four or five tutors who helped them to organise their work.

I visited the school on two separate occasions for three days each time, and I saw only one team, but I was immensely impressed by what I saw. The first thing that struck me when I entered the school was that the children behaved as if I was an ordinary human being; they were friendly and polite, but there was none of the artificial courtesy that occurs in highly disciplined schools. The teachers were known by their first names and there seemed to be no need for them to assert their authority. Here, too, there was an atmosphere of cordiality and an absence of awe.

What made all this different from Risinghill was that every child had an individual timetable, and it was not anticipated that any two timetables would be the same. These timetables were constructed in collaboration with tutors, and nearly all of them had extensive gaps in them, which were known as "team time." Team time included, among other things, all work in English and Social Studies, and in these areas the range of opportunity was infinite. The children wrote about what they wanted to write about and studied what they wanted to study, often outside the school altogether. Some of them seemed to do much of their work in the evenings, away from school, and to use the school mainly for social contact.

During one of my visits I assumed the role of a pupil, attending occasional classes and using team time for my own project, which was a study of the projects other students had chosen. I didn't want to interrupt people who were obviously engrossed in what they were doing, so I spoke to those who seemed less engaged, and I was astonished. It was hard to believe that this was a comprehensive school, with children from the whole ability range. They were without exception pleased with what they had done and proud to show it to me and to discuss it. That was a good beginning. But not only was the work interesting, it was also well-presented and extensive – far longer than any normal class project would be.

When Countesthorpe had started, with neither children nor staff familiar with the informal way it was run, there had been, as at Risinghill, a period of disorder and graffiti. By the time I visited it was a purposeful and peaceful place. There was no conflict between staff and pupils, and no truancy. Exam results were excellent, so good in English and Social Studies in particular that that one exam board is said to have sent down an inspector to make sure there was no cheating.

This happy place, with its success supported by statistics, was nevertheless soon forced back into a conventional mould by the appointment of a new head teacher, and staff-student conflict and truancy were re-established.

Room 13, Caol Primary School, 1993 –

Caol Primary School is in Fort William, within sight of Ben Nevis. Room 13 started with a visiting artist-in-residence called Rob Fairley, who spent only a few hours in the school each week. When I visited in 2004 and 2005 Rob was working full-time, and they had won a grant for £200,000 from NESTA, the National Endowment for Science, Technology and the Arts, to extend the present project from the one school where it already existed to three neighbouring primary schools and the local high school. The first artist-in-residence at the high school was Danielle Souness, an ex-pupil from Caol, and by 2010 there were new Room 13s in Glasgow, Nottingham, Eastbourne, Bristol, London, Nepal, Botswana, China, Turkey, South Africa and India.

Room 13 at Caol is an art room – just one room in an ordinary primary school. What makes it unique is that it is entirely under the control of the children who use it. They employ their own artist-in-residence, they have their own bank account and cheque book, they raised their own grant from NESTA, they buy their own materials, keep the books and deal with the correspondence. The art room is open all day, and anyone who has finished the work set by their teacher (or in the top group anyone who feels like a change) can leave the classroom and go up to Room 13. There they can paint, or read, or do administrative jobs, or borrow the camera, or work with the computers, or play chess, or chat with the staff or with each other.

The room is untidy. There are usually paintings stacked against the walls and lying on the floor. The floor is covered with paint spills. The sink is often full of dirty paint trays and brushes that have not been properly cleaned. It does not look like a classroom, it looks like an artist's studio.

And although some of the work resembles what is done in other school art rooms, a great deal of it is more like what is done in artists' studios. Room 13 has repeatedly won prizes for its work, and has exhibited at, among other places, Tate Modern, where many visitors assumed the paintings were done by adults. The children have also made a thirty-minute video about Room 13 which was shown on Channel 4.

Room 13 also differs from most primary classrooms in that it handles philosophical questions and allows children to discuss profound issues that matter to them, but that adults often feel they should be shielded from. What happens to the part of you that is you, when you die? How did it feel to be under the débris on 9/11? How are we going to use £200,000? When and how will the world end? Nikki Donnelly, aged 11, used photographs of dead animals in her work. Room 13 children have been to India and Nepal. They have climbed mountains in Scotland and been invited to go stalking and shoot and gralloch deer.

I have been there twice, for a total of nine days. The first time I could not properly digest what I saw, and the second time, although I understood somewhat better, one of the things that I understood was that Room 13 is in a perpetual state of change.

Although the staff are called Mr and Miss so-and-so, there is an atmosphere of equality, and the children expect to be treated with respect; after all, they are running a real business with substantial amounts of money. The management team, which consists entirely of children, meets regularly. Mr Fairley might come to the beginning of a meeting to explain some of the more difficult issues, but he would leave when the discussions began. There are times every day when there is no adult in the room, and the children carry on peacefully with whatever they were doing, without apparently noticing.

I asked a number of children why they came to Room 13, and the majority came either to do art work or to talk to the adults who might be there, but there were other reasons. Some came to do administrative work, but there were others who just wanted to get away from class or to avoid going out into the playground. When I asked them what they most valued about Room 13, though, the two top qualities were the feeling that they were respected, and above all the fact that in Room 13 they could do something real, not just school work.

To employ an adult who you pay with your own money, to paint pictures which go all the way to London for exhibitions, to handle dead animals, to see the poverty in India, to be taken seriously when you want to discuss the purpose of life, to express your fears, memories and delights in paint without adult interference, to make a television programme that is actually broadcast by a national network, these are experiences that lead to a self-confidence that cannot possibly be gained from lessons given by a teacher, however well-intentioned.

Why the Example is Not Followed

The stories of Risinghill and Countesthorpe give one reason why their examples were not followed, which is that when the schools began there was fairly serious disorder. The press loves stories of disorder, particularly when it is associated with ideas of freedom and independence. The word "anarchy" has been hijacked to mean chaos, when actually it means order without power. The first terms at Risinghill and Countesthorpe were held up as examples of the first sort of anarchy, and no one wanted to acknowledge that their later years were examples of the second.

When the Peckham Experiment started, the children raced all round the building and used the ashtrays for curling. When he first arrived at the centre, Brian O, aged 4, was "up to mischief". It demands a great deal of confidence for adults to refuse to take charge in such situations, but the problem was solved without repression. Michael Duane experienced a period of distressing disorder when he abolished corporal punishment at Risinghill, but he weathered the storm without resorting to other authoritarian measures, and the school settled into a new and healthier pattern. When Countesthorpe College started, students used to paint slogans on the walls and block the lavatories so that they flooded over. The staff patiently scrubbed off the graffiti and cleaned out the lavatories. By the time I visited, it was clean and decorous, and the working atmosphere was excellent.

Where things are already running smoothly, authority is not merely unnecessary but is actually damaging. The atmosphere at Countesthorpe was destroyed by the appointment of a new head teacher.

Unfortunately it is also true that when children are used to order being maintained by authority alone, then too swift a removal of authority results in temporary chaos. There is no publicity value in announcing that a school is clean and decorous. The initial period of disorder is what attracts media attention, and it is what the public remember.

Another reason that such schools cannot last is the hostility they attract from people who have given their lives to teaching in conventional schools and feel the suggestion that there might be a better way as a personal insult. Much of O'Neill's trouble at Prestolee, for instance, was caused by the indignant headmistress of the independent Infant Department.

And a third reason is that people who have suffered a conventional education believe it to have been important, and think it right to impose a similar suffering on today's children. This is the group that determinedly maintains that repressive discipline "never did me any harm"; they cannot see that even if it never did them any harm, it might have done a great deal of harm to others, and that "It never did me any harm" by no means rules out the possibility that "It never did me any good." "It never did me any harm" is a very weak recommendation.

Secondary state schools that show a proper respect for their students have never been allowed to continue doing so for long, but Prestolee was allowed to run successfully for over thirty years. Why has it been so ignored? And is there hope for Room 13?

I am afraid that Prestolee has been ignored because O'Neill wanted it to be. He had to make sure it kept a low profile if he was to be allowed to continue to run it as he thought right. He had problems with authority from time to time, and he did not want to set himself up as a target for authoritarians who believed that his successes must be illusory, because he was not conforming to the system. People feel safer with a familiar system that has been shown to fail than an unfamiliar one that has been shown to succeed. Conformity and irrational conscientiousness, to use the terms of Peck and Havighurst, are more powerful than rational altruism.

Room 13 has been making progress in an educational world that the government is trying to make increasingly repressive. As far as I know no one has tried to close a Room 13 down. Perhaps this is partly because each Room 13 is only one room in any given school. This means that it is not too frightening, and anyway it could be closed down at any moment if the head teacher thought it was having a bad influence. Luckily the head teacher at Caol, Jennifer Cattenach, is thoroughly supportive. When she was first appointed, she told me, Room 13 "was just so different, it was so exciting, so new. It was just – tingle factor." With her approval, the Room 13 atmosphere leaks out into the rest of the school.

Long may it continue to leak, long may Caol continue to be proud of its children who make videos for Channel 4 and exhibit their art in London. But it isn't because of the videos and the London exhibitions that Room 13 is so important. It is important because of the way it demonstrates that a cordial, unpressured atmosphere which allows to children to follow their own interests, and to "do real things" produces not only contentment, but also a sense of purpose and real achievement.

In the NCA Art News Magazine in 2002 there was an article by two twelve-year-olds from Caol, Danielle Souness and Kerrie Grant. This was the final paragraph:

> It would be really good to be in charge of our own education, as we
> have always had to go with adults thinking, and they don't do the work
> they make the rules for. This does NOT mean we do not want to
> learn, quite the opposite, we would like to find a way that would make
> learning better and we think we should be listened to a lot more.
> Adults often think we are more stupid and ignorant of what goes on in
> the world than we really are. We actually DO know what would work.

CHAPTER SEVENTEEN

SUDBURY VALLEY SCHOOL

Sudbury Valley School is in Framingham, Massachusetts. It was founded in 1968 by a group of parents who felt that the existing educational system would do their young children irreparable harm, and therefore decided to set up their own alternative. At Sudbury Valley the children were to decide for themselves exactly how they would spend their time. Each child was to be given entire responsibility for his or her own learning. There would be teachers available, but no timetable, no curriculum.

The school now has two hundred students between the ages of four and twenty, and is still run on the same principles.

There has never been any system of examination. Students who want a diploma when they leave the school only have to present a thesis defending the proposition that they are ready to take responsibility for themselves in the community at large. Not every thesis is accepted.

I have had the good fortune to read a collection of Sudbury Valley theses, and I have been given permission to quote from it, as long as the authors remain anonymous. (I have given them initials alphabetically, so that it is possible to follow when someone has been quoted more than once.) What follows is not adult guesswork, it is information at first-hand.

I have chosen mainly quotations from students who came to the school because they were suffering from various problems elsewhere. This is not because such students were in the majority. There were also plenty who had been in the school for years, but their contentment does not bring out the contrasts between Sudbury and conventional schools with the same vividness.

First I quote some of the problems.

When I first enrolled, I was basically fleeing from my old school, a "traditionally" run system. I had been no stranger to unpopularity there; in a school of approximately four hundred, I was *the* least popular. I'm not looking for sympathy, not anymore at least, because I have learned to realize that sympathy is something I neither need nor want, and other people have lived through worse anyway. No, my point is that when I arrived here, I was, emotionally, at ground zero, and I needed this school desperately. — A. B.

Before I came to Sudbury Valley I was a very unhappy person. I was introverted and completely oblivious to the outside world. I had no friends, and I didn't want any. I refused to go to public school [this is the United States, so the phrase 'public school' means what it says], and I wouldn't talk to anyone about what was bothering me. I spent a lot of time going to different counselors who tried to pry out my feelings. I resented those people and I became more introverted than I had ever been before. During this time I had become ill, and for three months I stayed at home where I locked myself in my room and spent my time reading, writing and watching television. At this time I was also having a lot of family problems. My parents were in the process of a divorce and I had decided to stop visiting my father completely. To make matters worse the school authorities came after my mother and forced her to put me back in the public school system. I started attending junior high two hours a day in a special program for problem children. I had one teacher and about seven counselors. I was considered a problem child, and being titled a problem, I believed it, putting my opinion of myself at a very low point. But after a while I couldn't stand even two hours a day of public school, so I flat out refused to go. The system had taken a noticeable toll on me, so my mother, against my father's wishes, took me out. My mother and I talked about private schools, and finally we decided to look into Sudbury Valley. – C. D.

I came to Sudbury Valley School two years ago January. I came, not because I had a baby, but because I had a baby my attitude towards school changed. For once I took my education seriously. – E. F.

I left my former school, Algonquin Regional High School, because I was failing basically every course offered. That even included gym, jewelry and study. I'm sure you're wondering how does one fail a study hall? The only explanation I have is not to show up. Each course is worth a certain amount of credits. 107 credits are required for graduation. Each time you missed a class, 1/6 of a credit would be deducted from 107. If you failed a course, 5 credits would be deducted. After 2 years of this cycle of failing and skipping classes, I left Algonquin with 18 credits, which is far below the freshman minimum standard. That's not all I left Algonquin with. I left Algonquin with virtually no self respect or self confidence which, in turn, I feel contributed to an eating disorder I developed. – G. H.

I came to SVS in the Spring of 1985. I just left a public school because I could not deal with the workload in the state I was in. Back then I had a drug problem. I was either stoned all the time or out looking to get stoned. The drugs did a lot to me; I didn't care about my personal looks and I didn't care about the damage I was doing to my body. I guess, at the time, I did them as a sort of rebellion. I didn't like being told by teachers in public school what to do and what I needed to learn. When I entered SVS I finally had the freedom to choose what I thought would be important to know in my life. – I. J.

I went to public school in Weston until I was twelve years old. It made me miserable from the time I was five. What I remember from an early age was being forced into a situation where I felt lost, scared and angry all day, five days a week. As I grew older I began to hate. I hated the system, the teachers and the other kids, and they hated me too. When I was about ten, I began to look for a way out. I couldn't take it any more, but my mother wouldn't provide any cover or support for my escape. In fact, she continued to force me to go. I began to hate her too, because it had always been an "Us and Them" situation, and she had chosen the system over me. Looking back on it now, I think she might have thought it was for my own good, but that doesn't change the effect of her actions.

In junior high school I lost my only friends because it was socially devastating for them to associate with me.

By the time I was in seventh grade, I began to actively resist the system rather than just resenting. it. After about two weeks I decided not to go any more, and at that point there was nothing my mother or anybody else could do about it. — K. L.

All these people left Sudbury Valley with diplomas. Many of the authors of the theses that I read described the way the school had helped them to change.

The place was gorgeous and the people there talked to me like I had never been talked to before. They talked to me as if I was a responsible individual. I was thrilled. Like so many others, I came in to SVS wanting to take all kinds of classes. That soon died off and I found myself doing what many others did. I hung out. I drank coffee and played hacky-sack. I talked to a lot of different people from little kids to staff members. All with the same kind of casual trust. I got to know people and feel comfortable in the school regardless of how long my stay would be. — M. N.

At first I spent my time talking to people and listening to music. I did this for about three months before I got real bored. So it was then I decided to try something new.

For Christmas I had been given a guitar and at school there was a very good instructor named George. I learned a lot from him in the six months I took guitar lessons. George was also the Executive Director of the Photography Corporation [Corporations at SVS are volunteer groups responsible for particular activities] and this was another thing that I was interested in. I got certified for developing film and making prints. Quickly I started taking pictures. I did this for almost a year and had lots of fun.

Then the next year at school I turned my sights towards something new. I had become interested in Law Enforcement. I found books at school and started reading them. Day by day I learned a lot about being a police officer. At this point I thought this is what I would be doing for a living.

But I finally decided that I would do what I had wanted to do since I was a kid.

I had always liked cars and enjoyed working on them. Since I was thirteen I had read "Hot Rod" magazines and other automotive literature. When I was fifteen I got my first car and worked on it till I started to drive. I had always had fun working on cars and found it real easy.

Then I looked into taking auto mechanics at school. There were a few books which I had read, but that wasn't enough. So I asked Dan Greenberg what I could do and Mimsy finally set up an internship so that I would be an apprentice to a very good mechanic named Tony Mauri, at a Sudbury garage close to school. – O. P.

When I entered SVS I finally had the freedom to choose what I thought would be important to know in my life. I also, for the first time in my life, had the freedom to do what I wanted as long as I followed the school's rules. It wasn't too hard. Soon after entering the school I quit doing drugs and started getting interested in things other than sex, drugs and rock and roll. (I am the first one to admit that sex and rock still play a part in my life, but they are not the only things that I think about.) For the first time I was looking into things that just looked interesting, like archeology. But when I found out it wasn't like Indiana Jones, I lost interest. Also, for a while, I tried film, but even though I still love it, it was too expensive a hobby for a sixteen year old to afford.

When I was younger I had a huge fascination with books. During my rebellious stage, I totally lost interest in reading. Anything that didn't have pictures and wasn't action-packed from page one was too much for me to read. At SVS I rediscovered books. I started reading my old favorites like J.R.R. Tolkien and Ray Bradbury. I found out they were much more fulfilling than Spiderman and soon found myself picking up books of all sorts, even some of the textbooks that are in the school. I can't say that I read them all the way through, but I read chapters that interested me. But my biggest love has always been fantasy. The exploits of those heroes was something I wished I could live. Recently I discovered that I can't live those lives, but I can do second best. I can create them. I started to write. I started by complete accident when my friend was putting together a magazine and told me that I should write something for it. I said I'll try. I sat down and wrote a story and actually enjoyed it. I started writing more often and, for a while, I got in the habit of writing every day. Now it is the one thing that I enjoy most. – I. J.

My mother did, in fact, get an interview at Sudbury Valley for me; but also prepared me for possible rejection once my records from Algonquin were reviewed by the staff. During the interview with Hanna [a Sudbury Valley staff member], to my surprise, she ripped up my records and told me that they weren't necessary here. I can't explain what a relief that was; I was actually getting accepted to a school without my previous records haunting me. – G. H.

The experiences described in the Sudbury students' diploma theses were enormously varied, but for children coming from other schools where they had failed the pattern was usually similar – first relief, as described by G. H., at not being judged by conventional school standards, then either idleness or false enthusiasm for traditional subjects followed by a period of readjustment and finally a discovery of personal objectives and an understanding of what the school can offer.

When people hear about schools like Sudbury for the first time, they are inclined to comment that of course the children are happy in such a friendly, free place, but do they ever learn anything? Some of the students I have already quoted have described how they took up, for instance, reading, writing, music or car mechanics. They found themselves motivated to learn because they were able to study what interested them. However, they did not see such learning as the most important benefit they had gained from the school. Over and over again they talked of acquiring a sense of purpose and a sense of personal worth.

> I decided if my life was ever going to be defined or even comprehensible I'd need to focus more on my politics and stop fiddling around with other things that compete for my time and attention. Hanging out was the first to go, but there are still things competing for my time. School is one of them. I'm always either missing political events and tasks or I'm missing school.
>
> Leaving school is very difficult for me because it's been one of the only dependable things I've ever known. I've always been able to come here, and there isn't any fear here. There's nothing to run from here, in fact this is where I've always run to, but being a student here just takes too much time and as much as I'd like to spend the rest of my life in a small isolated community with nothing to be afraid of, there are things going on in the outside world that scare me, and I feel I have to give priority to changing them. – K. L.

For closing words I just want to let the staff know what I feel are the most important things I got from the school, being:

1. Self-motivation: something I lacked a lot of until I came here.

2. A sense of timing, knowing when it's time to stop playing and get to work on what you want.

3. Responsibility: I think basically, responsibility means being able to decide for yourself what has to be done, putting it in a wise order of priority and following the order.

4. Good judgment: knowing what's right and wrong for me, myself, as a person, not for someone else who I would like to be seen as.

5. I think one of the most important things that I learned while I was here is that, not only were the kids and staff members here to guide me, teach me and discipline me, they also turned out to be some of my best friends. — Q. R.

When I started at SVS three years ago I had no idea about what I wanted to do. Since then I've changed so much that I'm practically a different person. I remember taking David Gould's psychology class and thinking that I had to find something to make myself a whole person. What I didn't know was that I am a whole person and I just needed to find confidence in myself. I've gone through so many changes since then. I've always been independent but I was shy and insecure and it was holding me back. Today I am more outgoing. confident and open minded than I ever was before. This is very important to me, more than anything else I have gotten out of Sudbury Valley. – *S. T.*

I've turned myself on to making music and learning through improvisation. I've learned to write more naturally and enjoyably. I've gained a better understanding of democracy and come to value the rights it empowers us with through direct experience. But most of all I've gained self confidence and contentment by learning to listen to myself. I know that I will be connected in some way to Sudbury Valley for the rest of my life and when I think back to my time here, I will think of how I learned one of the most important lessons of my life – how to be me. – *U. V.*

Most of these quotations have been from the theses of students who were only at Sudbury Valley for two or three years. I chose them in order to show that a school like this can help young people to recover from unsuccessful education elsewhere. It does not give a full picture of the school, which has students from the age of four. There are many theses from students who have been at the school for fourteen years, their entire school life. Sudbury Valley is not primarily a school for those who have been failed by the normal system, though it inevitably attracts a number of them; it is a school that allows all students to develop in ways that a traditional education blocks.

W. X., another rescued casualty who described his time at Sudbury Valley as a rebirth, said this:

While this was going on, I was learning; learning about people, learning how to interact. I didn't really start to learn these things until I came to Sudbury Valley School. Actually, that's not true. It was more like relearning something that I used to know.

It seems a shame that most schools teach children to forget.

CHAPTER EIGHTEEN

CONFIRMATION FROM OTHER SOURCES

In Chapters Nine and Ten I voiced, I hope without distorting them, a number of objections to my central proposals. In this chapter I shall do the opposite, and use a variety of sources to show the breadth of support for this kind of thinking. I shall refer to an ombudsman, two American teachers, a remedial teacher, a family therapist, a social entrepreneur, a table mat and a street child.

The Ombudsman

Målfrid Grude Flekkøy was the first Norwegian Ombudsman for Children, appointed in 1981. She was Ombudsman for eight years, and she wrote a book about her experiences (*A Voice for Children*, Jessica Kingsley Publishers). For eight years all her working life was concerned with children and issues that concerned children – the prohibition of physical punishment, traffic laws, play areas, locations of schools, television programming and so on. She also helped individual children, although she was not allowed to intervene in family disputes. She may fairly be considered to have been the expert with the widest knowledge of children's affairs of anyone in the world. I shall quote parts of two paragraphs from her concluding chapter, "Visions and Views", and I must stress that the crosshead between them, "Children have Superior Knowledge", is hers or her editor's, not mine.

If we try to think which personal qualities our young will need in the future, many of us will be uncertain. The world and its communities are changing so quickly that it is hard to say, for instance, what kinds of information children should be getting at school. Even computer languages taught in school today may be obsolete by the time the pupils leave school. Understanding and communication, between nations, different cultures and languages is increasingly important. Precisely because the world is changing so fast, young people must be creative, flexible, imaginative, understanding, responsible, caring and sharing, optimistic and peace loving. Reports from many countries, however, show a strong increase in suicides amongst young people, increasing depression, antisocial behaviour, drug abuse, hopelessness and pessimism, particularly about the future of a world threatened by nuclear destruction, pollution and overpopulation. These tendencies can be counteracted. If children share decision-making and responsibility, so that they feel they can make a difference, that they can help change things, within their family, their schools and their organisations, they grow up fighting for causes and believing in a better future.

Children have Superior Knowledge
Children should have the right to offer opinions, propose change and make mistakes doing so. If the possibility that mistakes might be made is a criterion for denying anybody the right to try, adults should not be allowed to try new ideas either. There are many opportunities for children and young people to take their part in decision-making processes – opportunities which are far too often denied them. In their family, in their neighbourhoods, in organisations and at school children very often not only have opinions, but superior knowledge. They know not only where the areas *planned* for play are, but the areas being used

(often not the ones the adults think). They know what equipment is available, and how much it is used. They know what they want to enrich the areas in which they spend time and learn. They have inside information about causes in school or organisational conflicts. They react soundly (and often loudly) to discrimination or unfair treatment, often seeing this when the adults are 'blind' to what is going on. They know, as 'consumers' what they like or dislike at school, in neighbourhoods, in organisations. Like anyone else they have to put up with some things they dislike, but that does not mean that, because they are small, they cannot understand reasons or that they cannot – in contrast to many adults – come up with ideas that could ameliorate the situation. Surveys have indicated that when the children are asked for advice and opinions about their surroundings, they usually come up with good ideas for improvement and soundly-based opinions. They may need advice about where to get information, how to present a proposal, which authority would be the right one, which channels they might use to get their views across. But the problem in implementing the suggestions often lies with the adults – first in listening, second in taking the children seriously, and finally, if the idea reaches that stage, in resources.

This may appear at first sight just to be a description of those areas where children have more relevant experience than adults, but as well as listing those areas, Flekkøy stresses the children's moral approach. When they are consulted, "they usually come up with good ideas for improvement and soundly based opinions." Social deterioration can be reversed, says Flekkøy, and if children have a genuine share in decision-making and responsibility and can really help to change things, they grow up "fighting for causes and believing in a better future." It is only when they feel disempowered that they do not pursue such aims.

The pace of change in technology since 1989 is illustrated by Flekkøy's reference to "computer languages taught in school". Children learn to use computers now, but they seldom learn to program them. The social problems she mentions, though, show no sign of abating, and to her list of threats to the world we now have to add global warming.

Two American Teachers

The conventional school system in the United States is in a bad way, with metal-detectors at the doors of some schools, and police in the school halls. The politicians have proposed methods of putting things right that are all too familiar in Britain – tighter discipline, a national curriculum, more testing, longer school days. Such remedies are no more effective there than they are here, and one of the results has been that one and a half million children are now educated at home by their parents.

There have also been plenty of small independent schools founded, with varying success and varying lengths of life. One of the early ones was The First Street School, which George Dennison describes in *The Lives of Children*. It was a school in the slums of New York which lasted for two years in the 1960s, had about twenty-three pupils and in that short time transformed the lives of several of them.

Here is one of the things George Dennison discovered while teaching there:

> That when the conventional routines of a school are abolished (the
> military discipline, the schedules, the punishments and rewards, the
> standardization), what arises is neither a vacuum nor chaos, but rather
> a new order, based first on relationships between adults and children,
> and children and their peers, but based ultimately on such truths of the
> human condition as these: that the mind does not function separately
> from the emotions, but thought partakes of feeling and feeling of
> thought; that there is no such thing as knowledge per se, knowledge in
> a vacuum, but rather all knowledge is possessed and must be expressed
> by individuals; that the human voices preserved in books belong to the
> real features of the world, and that children are so powerfully attracted
> to this world that the very notion of their curiosity comes through to
> us as a form of love; that an active moral life cannot be evolved except
> where people are free to express their feelings and act upon the insights
> of conscience.

This discovery was not made in a comfortable school for motivated middle class kids, it was made in a slum area where some of the children could not read at all, and for many of them, who were Puerto Rican, English was a second language. Even in such an environment as this, children have an active moral life, but it does not evolve unless it has the freedom to do so. Repressive measures do not reinforce moral attitudes; they actually inhibit moral development.

John Taylor Gatto, unlike George Dennison, worked within the conventional state system, and won awards as New York State Teacher of the Year in 1990 and 1991. Then, all of a sudden, he resigned from the government school system with a considerable flourish. This is part of what he said to justify his resignation:-

> Over the past twenty-six years, I've used my classes as a laboratory where *I* could learn a broader range of what human possibility is – the whole catalogue of hopes and fears – and also as a place where I could study what releases and what inhibits human power. During that time, I've come to believe that genius is an extremely common human quality, probably natural to most of us. I didn't want to accept that notion – far from it – my own training in two elite universities taught me that intelligence and talent distributed themselves economically over a bell curve and that human destiny, because of those mathematical, seemingly irrefutable, scientific facts, was as rigorously determined as John Calvin contended. The trouble was that the unlikeliest kids kept demonstrating to me at random moments so many of the hallmarks of human excellence – insight, wisdom, justice, resourcefulness, courage, originality – that I became confused. They didn't do this often enough to make my teaching easy, but they did it often enough that I began to wonder, reluctantly, whether it was possible that being in school itself was what was dumbing them down. (from *Dumbing Us Down*)

The destruction of insight, wisdom, justice, resourcefulness, courage and originality is more than just dumbing down – it is a systematic crippling of moral character. When people complain about the behaviour of young people nowadays, as they have always done since the ancient Greeks and probably long before then, they fail to see that it is the behaviour of the adults that has been the original cause.

The Remedial Teacher

The Swiss teacher, Jürg Jegge, expresses this idea in greater detail. He has described his work as a remedial teacher in two of his books, *Dummheit ist Lernbar (You can learn to be stupid)* and *Angst macht krumm (Fear screws you up)*. Neither has been translated into English, in spite of their enormous success in the original German. He worked much of his life in remedial classes and in one of a group of extremely small schools (Schulen in Kleingruppen) where children who had been rejected, even by other special schools, could find a refuge. Then he set up a group called Der Märtplatz (Swiss dialect for "The Market-place") where at any one time twenty people between the ages of 16 and 30 have the chance to take informal apprenticeships and at the same time expand their cultural horizons and restore their damaged personalities.

This is a list of some of the problems he had had to deal with in schools, as he listed them in *Dummheit ist Lernbar*: "inability to concentrate, restlessness, nervousness, weakness in reading, weakness in mathematics, disturbs lessons, has problems with abstract thinking appropriate for his (or her) age-group, IQ well below average, little social sense, an out-and-out loner, a minor delinquent, has outbreaks of violence, slightly wayward, perpetual role-playing, sleep problems, bed-wetting, definitely disturbed behaviour, often absent, a dreamer, sniffs glue, smokes a lot of hashish, etc."

Jürg Jegge's great message is that no child deliberately develops any of these problems, no child wants to be a trouble-maker, a liar or a bully, but that once you have been labelled as stupid, dishonest or insolent, or what-ever it may be, then you have to live up to your reputation. If you are additionally handicapped by a home with little or no affection and a culture virtually limited to television game shows, all you can do in an ordinary school setting is put a brave face on your misery and contribute to your own decline.

He tells many stories of the distress caused to his pupils by teacher's criticisms; of the little boy punished for going to help himself to a present from the Christmas tree at his nursery school, when he hadn't understood that everyone was taking turns; of the boy who spent an evening trying to learn his spellings with the help of his sister, whose test was returned to him the next day with the comment, "If only you had done some work on this at home you might have done better;" of the girl who was moved to a new school bringing a bad reputation with her, and was always assumed to be the culprit when anything went wrong – a rubber was stolen, or the blackboard was scribbled on; of the boy called Peter Good who was nearly always at the end when the class was made to stand in order after a test, and of whom the teacher said, to the amusement of the whole class, that he ought to be called "Peter Bad."

When Jegge tells such stories to adults, they say that they too remember such incidents, and indeed he remembers being treated the same way himself, but these were isolated experiences. The children he had in his care had faced such criticism hour after hour, day after day. "Already in the kindergarten," wrote one boy, "I had learnt that there was something destructive, wicked about me. I had been told so about a thousand times. Now an idea suddenly occurred to me. If I really had such an evil character, why shouldn't I behave like that?" The girl mentioned above, who had the bad reputation, wrote, "And the worst thing was that I always felt guilty, even when I hadn't done it. I got every sort of talking-to when I got worse at things. And I did get worse. I got worse in arithmetic, worse in language, worse in singing, and then I really began to steal, smoke and lie, and got lower and lower marks."

Jegge showed that by building up the self-confidence of young people like this, offering them wide cultural and social experience and above all treating them with affection and respect, he could help them to develop their repressed abilities and live up to their own moral standards, the standards that their teachers had told them were unattainable. With his support children who had learnt illiteracy and delinquency in their conventional schools, became literate and responsible.

The Family Therapist

Jesper Juul, a Danish family therapist, former director of the Kempler Institute of Scandinavia and the Family Counseling International in Croatia, is even blunter in his distribution of blame for children's "bad" behaviour. "When children cease to co-operate," he says, "it is either because they have co-operated too much for too long, or because their integrity has been harmed. It is *never* because they are unco-operative." (My italics)

This quotation is from the only one his books available in English, *Your Competent Child*, published in the USA. (He is unhappy about the English title: children do not belong to their parents, he says; the title should have been *The Competent Child.*)

The children who were sent to Jegge had mostly had their integrity virtually destroyed, and their misbehaviours were a twisted sort of co-operation: their teachers said they were stupid, or lazy, or dishonest, so stupid or lazy or dishonest they must be. Juul lays the responsibility at the door of the parent rather than the teacher, but at the same time exonerates the parent because the mistakes parents make are largely the result of the way they themselves were brought up. Jegge agrees that parents are part of the problem, but that they know no better; teachers, he says, are employed to know better, and he holds them to have failed in their duty.

Juul regards moral education as a contradiction in terms. Trying to train children to do what they ought to do often has the opposite effect.

> When children are brought up to be aware of their social responsibility, they often become socially responsible. In fact, many of them become what I would describe as over-responsible. Unfortunately, these socially overdeveloped people often lack personal responsibility, either completely or partially. On the other hand, when children are brought up to develop their natural, personal responsibility, they also tend to become highly socially responsible as a part of this process. This phenomenon completely contradicts one of the bedrock beliefs about how to bring up children – that their "egocentric nature" must be repressed out of consideration for the larger community. It also contradicts the beliefs of those who assume that it is necessary to compromise one's own integrity in order to be of value to one's community.

"When children have to choose between their own integrity and co-operating," says Juul in another context, " – and this happens to them, as it does to adults, scores of times every day – children choose co-operation nine times out of ten." He then goes on to say that adults do not normally pay much attention to children's behaviour when they co-operate. "Only when our children stop or refuse to co-operate do we sit up and take notice." It is only because adults are so unobservant that the high motivation of children is unrecognised.

Juul also stands up energetically for teenagers:

> Viewed objectively, puberty is an intrapsychic (that is, it takes place within the individual), psychosexual period of development that causes many twelve-to-fifteen-year-olds to experience internal uncertainty and turbulence. The idea that this development should in itself cause interpersonal conflicts with adults is rubbish.

And:

> The notion that adolescence in itself is the cause of conflicts with parents is a myth. Primarily, conflicts arise because parents lack the will or the ability to recognise and engage with the unique and independent person that their child is in the process of becoming.

Parents are afraid that this unique and independent person, if allowed to surface, will revert to some primitive egoism, whereas in fact repression may result in rebellion, and freedom will result in co-operation and social responsibility. Juul summed up this view in the following three sentences:

- Children who are treated with respect treat others with respect
- Children who are cared for care for others
- Children whose integrity is not violated don't violate the integrity of others

I was particularly delighted to find this, because in an early prospectus for Sands School I had written:

- Children who are trusted will become trustworthy
- Children who are respected will learn a proper self-respect
- Children who are cared for will learn to care for others

Later I changed this, because I felt it was describing a therapeutic process, which in ideal conditions would not be necessary. The new version was grammatically further from Juul's, but closer in meaning: "Children are trustworthy unless they have not been trusted. Children have a proper self-respect as long as others have respected them. Children care for others unless they have not been cared for themselves." Juul's version is briefer, clearer and stronger. He doesn't bother with words like "unless".

Another example of his welcome certainty is the use of the word "always" in this passage:

In relationships between children and adults, adults are *always* [my italics] responsible when violence erupts. This does not just apply to those cases in which the adults use violence, but also to those in which children or young people behave violently toward their parents, brothers and sisters, friends, and strangers, and to property belonging to their immediate family or to other people.

In recent years, politicians from all over the world have come forward to condemn the violent actions of children and young people. With the support of outraged and indignant parents, they have made demands for harsher punishment. This strategy is beyond absurd. It is about as ludicrous as the suggestion that we should pay off the national deficit with Monopoly money.

Partly as a result of the liberalization of society and the increasing self-awareness among children and young people, a terrifying number of them express their pain publicly and destructively. This development will continue until we begin to assume responsibility for the massive violence, both physical and psychological, that adults still express toward children.

The Social Entrepreneur

Camila Batmanghelidjh was named Social Entrepreneur of the Year in 2005 for her work with those children mentioned by Juul who express their pain publicly and destructively. She is the founder of Kids Company, which provides therapeutic and social help to approximately 4,500 children across London through schools, and a centre offering a concentrated service for about 600 children who come directly from the streets every year. Many of these are the children who are so often thought to be a proof that evil is a natural consequence of lack of discipline – the hoodies, the young prostitutes, the muggers, the gang members, the juvenile drug addicts and thieves. "No child," says Batmanghelidjh in her book, *Shattered Lives*, "is born a criminal and a killer – something happens to generate hate in them." She describes a few of these 'somethings,' and they are appalling. Many of the children's homes are stinking, filthy and chaotic. Many of the parents are violent. Some children have had to steal in order to eat. Batmanghelidjh tells of a family who were secretly fed by a neighbour who dropped food through the letter-box, too afraid to approach the mother directly. Many of the parents were addicted to drugs, and some used drugs to calm their babies. Some forced their own children into prostitution. One twelve-year-old who was caring for three younger siblings because her mother either ignored or beat them, resorted to, as she describes it in the book, "sucking dicks for money" in order to be able to buy food. Nearly all these children have lived in such despair that they have considered suicide. The violence some of them direct at society may be no worse than the violence they exercise against themselves through self-harm and wildly dangerous behaviour.

This is Batmanghelidjh's account of the process:

Children physically terrorized describe other annihilating horrors. The body stores the blows, holds the score and remembers the sores. Children left to manage their bleeding vaginas and anus after unwanted penetration. Children choking with adult needs for sexual gratification. Rage and reactions combine – fury waiting for expulsion. Horrors of physical abuse never fade. The memory is played back in flashbacks; time and time again the terror relentlessly repeating, now as if then. In children who have been abused there is the urge for revenge. The hate is outward-bound towards the victim and/or inward-directed towards the self. It is the expression of murdered childhoods."

These children have been failed not only by their own parents, but also by the social system. Batmanghelidjh tells what struggles she has had even to find places for some of these children to live. The damage done by the parents is augmented by the rejection of society.

What is astonishing is how much of their original dignity and moral sense many of the children have managed to retain. Batmanghelidjh puts it like this:

> I have wondered about these children's sense of profound poetry. Their eloquence, their charm, their extraordinary dignity despite so much damage. How do they manage to keep their spirits so special? I feel lucky and privileged to be working with them. I love their honesty in hate and love. They are not flawed. They simply reflect back our own emotional and social flaws.

The Table Mat

All the time I have been writing this book I have felt that it has been necessary to protect myself against a general public hostility to the kind of views I have been expressing. It is therefore particularly surprising to find that the following poem has been given away with baby-foods and sold by the thousand in many different versions, including mini-posters and even table mats. Perhaps public opinion has been on my side all along.

Children Learn What They Live

If children live with criticism, they learn to condemn.

If children live with hostility, they learn to fight.

If children live with fear, they learn to be apprehensive.

If children live with pity, they learn to feel sorry for themselves.

If children live with ridicule, they learn to feel shy.

If children live with jealousy, they learn to feel envy.

If children live with shame, they learn to feel guilty.

If children live with encouragement, they learn confidence.

If children live with tolerance, they learn patience.

If children live with praise, they learn appreciation.

If children live with acceptance, they learn to love.

If children live with approval, they learn to like themselves.

If children live with recognition, they learn it is good to have a goal.

If children live with sharing, they learn generosity.

If children live with honesty, they learn truthfulness.

If children live with fairness, they learn justice.

If children live with kindness and consideration, they learn respect.

If children live with security, they learn to have faith in themselves and in those about them.

If children live with friendliness, they learn the world is a nice place in which to live.

— Dorothy Law Nolte, Ph.D.

I have divided the poem in two, separating the negative and positive characteristics. The reason for this is that I don't believe the positive characteristics have to be learnt; they exist unless they are eradicated. The "ifs" are not conditions for the learning of these good qualities, but for their survival. I hope that this small change will not lose me the support of the many good people who have admired this poem.

The Street Child

The following passages are extracts from the talk given at the 2000 International Democratic Education Conference in Tokyo by Amin, a fourteen-year-old street child.

My name is Amin. I have come on behalf of the Child Workers' Union, from the capital of India, that is Delhi. I want to speak on behalf of the child workers in Delhi, and I want to start more particularly about the street children in Delhi. Children come on the streets because of various reasons. Some because of the conflict in the family. Families break down, and that's why they come, and some come because they don't have enough work. We work hard on the streets, but in spite of that we face a lot of problems. We are harassed by the police, we need to look for space in the night to sleep on the street, and there are times when people, the general public, really look down upon us.

. . .

Although we work hard, we are often defined as kids, or often defined as brats by the people on the streets and there are times when you are really looked down upon and insulted and the police are blaming us for crimes we have not committed.

. . .

In the Union when some children that are in problems the other children help because they discuss their problem there. There is a kind of brotherhood, there is a kind of comradeship among us, and we are all part of the society so when we help each other and we discuss our problems . . . that makes us much more concerned for the collective problem of the society.

. . .

Very recently, that's one and a half years back in our country there was a war with Pakistan, and in the place called Kargill, that was where the war was taking place, and lots of people were dying, but the most affected population were the children of both the places in the villages, and in the union they discussed about it and we thought that it was important that we should be with the children of that area who were getting affected by the war and we collected money to send it to the children of both the countries.

After his talk he was asked a number of questions. One person asked how he got the confidence to speak as he did, and what he would do if he was given a large sum of money. This was his reply:

I live on the street, and by living on the street I get the confidence. But you must remember that when first a child comes on the street, he doesn't – he is not able, he is not that powerful, he will not be able to speak in that way, but once he starts living on the street he starts fighting for his life, fighting for his survival, that gives him the power. And that is education for him, to be able to speak for himself. And when you talk of money, I am a working child and I value my labour. Even if you were to give me a lot of money I would not take it. I am proud of the work I am doing.

This boy, who would refuse a gift of money because he was proud of the work he was doing, and who had donated money to help the children of Kargill, was earning about 30 rupees a day, barely enough to survive on. Looked down on, insulted and wrongly accused, he yet felt he was part of a brotherhood of people who not only helped each other, but were also concerned about general social problems. I have spent a week with Butterflies, the organisation for street children that he now works for, and I know that his attitudes are not exceptional.

The other sections in this chapter have all been based on the opinions of adults, experts on youth at second hand. Amin speaks from the front line.

CHAPTER NINETEEN

STRENGTH IN WHAT REMAINS BEHIND

Though nothing can bring back the hour
Of splendour in the grass, of glory in the flower,
We will grieve not, rather find
Strength in what remains behind.

William Wordsworth

Not Far Enough

Chapters Fourteen, Fifteen and Sixteen were about situations in which children were free to develop in accordance with their own inclinations. The children flourished, and retained or regained a natural sensitivity to other people's needs, and a wish to help to meet them. The adults involved knew that listening to children with respect was one of the most important ways of helping them to develop.

This is admirable, but it does not go far enough. The next step is to realise that listening to children with respect is one of the most important ways of learning how the world can be made a better place. Let me remind you of the words of my discovery as I wrote them in Chapter Eight. "Adults do not pass moral values on to their children; the best they can do is to relearn from their children the values that they themselves once held. In moral matters, children are better judges than grown-ups."

Even educators and psychologists who appear to support my views, often go no further than acknowledging that children have great moral sensitivity. They do not usually state that this moral sensitivity is diminished or even absent in most adults.

It is important to be clear that there is nothing naïve about this declaration. As I have shown time and again, there is evidence to support it. (I might add that the assertion that most adults have diminished moral sensitivity might be regarded as cynical rather than naïve.) There is confirmation even in the last three chapters, which were not specifically concerned with morality. Babies love their mothers with a "determined and unshakeable passion *unequalled in human relationships*," says Penelope Leach; adults find it hard to show "physical altruism" and to swing and chase freely in a gymnasium without crashing into one another, as the children at the Peckham Centre did so effortlessly; Amin was scornful of the adult who suggested that he might accept money that he had not earned. Few of us who have passed the age of twenty-five would dare to say with K. L., the Sudbury Valley student, "There are things going on in the outside world that scare me, and I feel *I have to give priority to changing them.*"

Adults are handicapped by declining faculties, both physical and mental, and by subservience to a wide variety of institutions. If you ask, "At what age is it right to start listening to children's views on moral questions?" the answer is, "As soon as they can express them." If you ask, "At what age is it right to stop listening to adults' views on moral questions?" the answer is, "As soon as they have learnt to ignore them."

I do not wish to suggest that as the years go by adults just become increasingly weak, senile and useless. Adults are powerful, and they have gained knowledge and experience. However, instead of putting this power, knowledge and experience into the service of the ideals that their children still understand, they put them into the service of institutions whose object is not the welfare of individual human beings, but their own survival as institutions. A value system has been created by our civilisation in which conforming is more important than caring, and this is at the root of injustice in the world.

Institutions appear to be selfish, rather like Richard Dawkins' genes. Dawkins even denied the possibility of the existence of an altruistic gene, yet I have shown that his theory suggests that though the idea of an altruistic gene is indeed nonsense, there is likely to be a gene for altruism. An institution can no more be selfish or altruistic than a gene.

We are made up of genes, and we form ourselves into institutions. Analysis of the theory of the selfish gene rather surprisingly leads to the idea of a gene for altruism, but examining the theory of the selfish institution, in contrast, only suggests a gene for stupidity.

It is only by rejecting institutional values – patriotism, conformity, respect, obedience – and substituting personal ones, such as empathy, friendship, altruism and care that we have any chance of making the world a happier and a fairer place. Children have not yet been infected by the institutional virus; we must learn to appreciate their health.

This should not be impossible. As the authors of *How Babies Think* say:

> Although we may not be as smart as babies are, the new evidence
> suggests that we may be smarter than we sometimes think. The reason
> we don't learn more may be exactly because we have already learned so
> much. The wiring we acquired in childhood literally as well as
> metaphorically tells us most of what we need to know, it works
> staggeringly well most of the time, and we are designed in a way that
> makes those successful programs difficult to change. Even as adults,
> however, when we face new problems, unexpected environments or
> unusual inputs, we seem to be able to change the wiring once more.

The Elephant on the Roof

Long before the expression "the elephant in the room" had turned into a cliché, Brian Patten wrote a poem called *The Experiment*. This experiment was conducted by a child to prove that groan-ups (sic) don't pay much attention to kids. After finding that the reaction of two different groan-ups to a couple of harmless but impossible remarks – 'That rabbit over there's just eaten a mouse' and 'The cat's just cooked itself some dinner' – was just 'Well I never,' the experimenter

> . . . dashed outside of the house yelling,
> 'There's an elephant just about to fall off the roof.'
> And they both said
> 'Well I nev – 'SPLAT!!!!

There is an elephant just about to fall off the roof and we had better listen. Many children have been so thoroughly humiliated by the small degree of attention they receive at home and at school that they have given up drawing attention to it, or have even come to believe that the elephant they have seen is a hallucination. Most adults know that the elephant hasn't fallen off yet, and they hope it never will, so they try not to think about it.

Children are not so indifferent. The concluding words of Sheila and Celia Kitzinger's book, *Talking with Children about Things that Really Matter*, underline this.

> Many adults feel baffled, frustrated and overwhelmed by the scale of human suffering. We may feel powerless to change anything. When we communicate that sense of helplessness and futility to children they become frightened and bewildered. Most children want to *do* something – they want to send money, help the victims, and alleviate suffering. They want to complain or protest, they want to ensure that injustice is not perpetuated. Instead of communicating apathy and helplessness, we can nurture children's developing understanding and their critical consciousness about political issues. We can encourage a sense that what they do *matters* – that they can make a difference. The most valuable message we can offer children is that they too can be active participants in the struggle to create a better world.

The trouble is that most of us have given up; we feel that telling children that they can make a difference is like encouraging them to believe in Father Christmas.

Trond-Viggo Torgerson, as Norwegian ombudsman for children in 1990, produced a booklet, *Facts about Children in Norway*, which has a section on children's concerns about the future. This is part of what he has to say about children and young people between 11 and 18.

In the mid-1980s, children and young people aged 11 to 18 were most worried about

- nuclear weapons

- unemployment

- drugs

From the mid-1980s up to the present time, it seems as though children have become increasingly concerned with pollution, environmental issues and AIDS.

It is the youngest children (11-13 years old) who are most alarmed about nuclear weapons, and their anxiety about nuclear arms diminishes as they grow older. The few studies available seem to indicate that girls are more worried about nuclear weapons than boys, and that boys are somewhat more concerned with pollution problems. The most important and perhaps the most interesting aspect is information about how children and young people tackle their knowledge of social problems, and the kind of feelings this knowledge arouses in them.

Their reactions are classed in five main categories:

1. Optimism

Children who say they are optimistic about their own future and that of the world, even though they list a number of worries and make many pessimistic statements.

2. Pessimism

This group of children expresses grave and profound concern about the chance of peace and future life on earth.

3. Hope of action

These children express deep concern, but at the same time believe that they themselves can work with others to do something about the situation.

4. Powerlessness

These children are well informed, but feel that they personally can do nothing about the threats they know exist to our earth and their own future.

5. Repression

The children say that they are unable/unwilling to think about threats to their own future, and that they repress any feelings and reactions they may have concerning important social problems. Some say that it is easy to repress this knowledge, while others must make an effort to do so "in order to avoid going insane."

Adults may fall into any of these five categories too, but the majority of us fall into categories 2, 4 and 5, the categories of despair. When a child tells us there is an elephant about to fall off the roof all we can say is "Well I nev –'

How to Hide an Elephant

Those who created the British national curriculum did not attach much importance to current affairs, politics or social problems. Then the Labour government elected in 1997 decided to introduce the theme of citizenship. A few schools have interpreted this as an indication that school pupils should have a more effective voice. In a very few of these few, children have been honestly consulted about many issues of importance to them, such as homework, the appointment of new staff, behaviour issues and even the school development plan, but in most schools the pupils only learn about citizenship, they are not to be allowed to practise it. That will have to wait until they are eighteen, when they will be allowed to vote in an election every once in a while.

Social issues of the kind that often concern the children directly, such as poverty, unemployment, sex-discrimination, crime, and racism are considered to be less important than a knowledge of procedures. Global warming, road-building, animal rights, genetically modified crops and even as remote a subject as the relief of Third World debt are of real concern to many young people, but they are not part of most conventional school programmes. When children organised protests against the Iraq war, teachers from some schools joined in, but in other schools they punished the demonstrators for truancy.

Put crudely, this means that in school children must learn about how society is governed, but if they want to learn about society itself they must do so independently. It is as if the curriculum were constructed deliberately to discourage children from finding out about the world around them. What might they do if they found out what the world was really like before they had understood the need to conform?

The first way to hide an elephant is to persuade everybody to look in the opposite direction. (That seemed to be the Bush administration's attitude to global warming, a problem already identified in the children's appeal to world leaders at the UN Conference on Environment and Development in Rio de Janeiro in 1992.)

The second way is to laugh at anyone who claims to have seen it.

Teachers learn not to take their pupils' opinions seriously. Test your own reaction to this true story, which was much repeated in the staff-room of a certain school. A twelve-year-old boy who had been in trouble was brought before the head to be cross-examined. He was told that all the teachers were fed up with him, and asked whether he could name any teacher who would have a good word for him. He named his class-teacher, and when he was asked why she would speak up for him, he said, "Because she respects me."

How have you reacted? The teacher in question was delighted when she heard that her respect had been appreciated. However, the reason that the story was being repeated among the staff was that the child's observation was so amusingly absurd.

If you have no respect for children of course it is foolish to listen to them. If you yourself haven't seen the elephant for years because you have always looked in the wrong direction, then no amount of warning from a child can make any difference to you.

Systematically, Conscientiously, Blindly Wrong

The elephant is there, and it is desperately urgent that we do something about it, yet adults, who have almost all the power, use that power systematically, conscientiously, blindly in the wrong directions.

When children break windows or steal packets of sweets they know they are doing wrong; when a grown man evicts a tenant who can't pay the rent, or complains about the unemployed getting money for nothing, or shouts at his child for staying out late, or puts up prices to increase dividends, he believes that what he is doing is right. Indeed, in our society's terms it *is* considered right, just as in some societies it is considered right that two-year-old girls should have their clitorises cut out and their vaginas sewn up, or that young men should have patterns carved in their faces so that they can show their endurance, or that thieves should have their hands cut off, or that adulteresses should be stoned to death.

In western civilisation our customs may have become less savage on a personal level, but on an institutional level we have carried out horrors that would have been impossible for less developed nations – the gassing of the Jews, Hiroshima and Nagasaki, Dresden, the use of napalm in Vietnam and white phosphorus in Iraq. These were the crimes of adults, and the adults who performed them believed that what they were doing was right.

On a more domestic level, consider the relative suffering that would be caused by two imaginary incidents. In the first, a burglar breaks into a house and steals jewellery worth a million pounds. In the second, a Chancellor of the Exchequer reduces benefits to the poorest people in the country in order to cut taxes for the rich. There can be no question but that the second causes more suffering, yet there is no law against it. If you believe that the important thing is to obey rules, you will think that the burglar has committed the worse crime; if you believe in the importance of maximising happiness and minimising suffering, then the Chancellor of the Exchequer is the greater criminal.

This kind of issue is absolutely clear to children. Their primary moral concern, as I have shown, is not even fairness, but a desire that everyone should be all right. We work hard to teach them to disdain their natural judgement, and by the time they are adults they have learnt to subordinate it to the requirements of the institutions to which they belong, and to demand that others do likewise. They do this because they believe it is in their own interest. Adolescents may well be confused, because they are having to change from one value-system to another. The adult view, when they finally accept it, is clear and consistent. It is also wrong.

An excuse for this twisting of morality is that our society is built on the manipulation of self-interest, and it is feared that if people suddenly become altruistic and selfless then society will collapse because there would be no way to control them. We have learnt that we have to behave in certain ways in order to earn enough to buy the latest electronic hardware or to go on exciting holidays. If we suddenly decided that we did not want two TVs, a CD player and a mobile phone that took photographs, and were quite happy to go on camping holidays or visit our friends, then there would be no way to make us work harder and the economy would collapse, causing universal suffering.

This excuse is based on the pessimistic, cynical and inaccurate view that people only work in order to gain material reward. In fact they work for companionship, for routine and above all for dignity and a sense of usefulness. If we lost interest in maximum material gain, society would certainly change, and it would change for the better. The reason we cannot bear to consider change is that we have been brain-washed into believing that the preservation of our institutions is more important than the welfare of the people within them.

We have also learnt a respect for power that goes beyond mere obedience. We obey our institutions without any commands being given; we believe that we are behaving naturally. It seems natural to submit to power. We are even prepared to believe that people who are powerful are also right, because they could not otherwise have become powerful. In times of political crisis we are inclined obey leaders with an almost insane loyalty.

And we also believe in the corresponding point of view, that anyone who has no power is unimportant and is likely to be wrong. This accounts for a lack of respect for the unemployed, for the Third World and for children, and it accounts for some men's lack of respect for women.

Power is not evidence of being right. It is a matter of folk-wisdom that all power corrupts. The catastrophic environmental problems caused by powerful institutions are evidence of this. When we think we are virtuously submitting to authority we are abandoning our own convictions for no morally justifiable reason.

Children have a natural morality that is superior to the institutional morality adopted by adults. Neither children nor adults always behave according to their own moral guidelines. The trouble is that for adults the moral guidelines themselves are wrong.

The Enormous Difficulty of Change

Adults fear change. They are afraid to take children's opinions seriously. When there is a difference of opinion between adults and children they believe they are always right and the children are always wrong. They think that to abandon this position would be to reverse it, so that they would always be wrong and the children would always be right. They have overlooked the possibility of discussion.

The explanation given by Kristin Eskeland, the founder of the Voice of the Children, was that adults could not take children's concerns seriously because the changes necessary would be too painful. Yet we must hope that adults are going to be brave enough to bear the pain, so that the world is capable of change.

It is considered astonishing that the USA elected Bill Clinton as president when he was still under fifty years old, but no nation has fifty-year-olds representing it at the Olympic Games. There is a law that says that the president of the United States cannot be younger than 36. I would like to see a law that all heads of state retire at thirty, and become supportive civil servants to the young idealists who succeed them.

One of the reasons we are frightened of giving power to the young is that we remember our own youthful mistakes with embarrassment, and feel we know better now. I certainly feel like that myself. I have no evidence from my childhood, but I have a diary that I kept on and off from the age of 20 until the age of 24. It is full of snobbery, anxieties about girl-friends, ignorance and conceit, and yet I found in it the statement of the theme of this book that I mentioned in Chapter One. (I didn't want you to read it then, but if you want to read it now, it is in Appendix Two.)

I also found the following passages that I wrote when I was twenty-four. They exemplify the moral directness of the young, and the second paragraph gives a further cogent explanation for the reluctance of the old to change their minds.

Liking people for their intellect, or their social standing, or their appearance, is only legitimate if you love them for their humanity too. And by humanity I mean little more than their existence – you must love a man simply because he is there.

. . .

It seems that as people get older, they gain in knowledge and experience but their views get narrower, and their conviction that they are right grows. They become settled in their ways. This is obviously potentially a good thing, if the position their youth has led them to is a good one, but very few people do in fact arrive at the best position. When you are settled in your ways you don't have to dispute with yourself every decision you make, and so save your conscience. If anyone questions your values then you become much angrier than a young person does, not because you have given more thought to them but because you have done such a lot as a result of them. You are attached to your beliefs not so much because your belief is any stronger, but because if your beliefs turn out to be wrong, your whole life has been wrong. That is why people produce such cunning arguments in favour of nepotism, snobbery, business ethics, etc.

This led me on to wonder what I consider is the basis of moral judgements, what is the right thing to do in life. It seems to me at first that one should have two aims – to do all one can to aid humanity to material and spiritual prosperity, and to develop oneself as far as possible towards the ideal of Jungian perfection, that is to say complete self-knowledge and maximum development of the four faculties. These two aims can each be expressed in terms of the other: you develop yourself in order to be able to help other people better: you help other people in order to develop yourself in the right directions.

Everyone's attitude to everyone else should be one of loving, humble *protectiveness*.

I would not wish the young man I was then to take the place of the old man I am now, even if such a thing were possible. I do not agree exactly with everything he says, and I have no longer any clear picture of the ideal of Jungian perfection. The young man did not know what I know now, he had little experience of teaching or organising, he had not been married, he had not had children of his own, he had no acquaintanceship with death. He had already been drilled to conform, and his departures from conformity were often superficial. Yet he knew things that I am only just rediscovering now.

What I would wish is that the idealism and energy and sensitivity and freshness and intelligence of the younger man should be able to work in combination with the experience and knowledge of the older man, so that we could complement each other and produce a figure very much more effective than either of us could be on our own. The proper relationship between young and old is not one of teacher and pupil, or authority and obedience, but of co-operation, affection and mutual appreciation. We need to learn to use the skills acquired with age to serve the needs sensed by youth.

We have come to expect that every day in every way we should get better and better. Actually in many ways we are getting recognisably worse and worse, both physically and in terms of mental agility. This decline is undeniable in the world of sport, but in the world of intelligence it tends to be ignored. The brilliant satirists are mostly young, computer programmers are young, mathematical geniuses do their best work when they are young, but the notion of mental decline is so much resented that most of us deny it. Psychologists like Reuven Feuerstein and Michael Shayer have tried to invent the mental equivalent of the exercise bike to prove that it doesn't have to happen. Student text-books on psychology have hundreds of pages on the development of intelligence, but usually not more than a page on its decline.

If there is such a strong reaction against believing that we are less intellectually lively than we were, in spite of the evidence, people are going to find it extremely hard to accept that they are less morally lively than they used to be. Yet the general acceptance of either or both of these truths would be of enormous value to mankind. Instead of trying to suppress the intelligence and insight of the young, we could work with them.

We Will Grieve Not

In many respects, though not all, we, as individuals, are not as good as we were. This becomes a less depressing thought if we can think of our whole lives as a single narrative. What I wrote in my diary when I was twenty-four is at least as important as what I am writing now. Perhaps it is more important. I need to learn respect for my former identity, and not to cringe with embarrassment when I remember things I did then that I would not do now. There are things I do now that make young people cringe.

Marcel Proust expressed a similar idea in *In a Budding Grove*:

There is hardly a single action we performed in that phase [adolescence] which we would not give anything, in later life, to be able to annul. Whereas what we ought to regret is that we no longer possess the spontaneity which made us perform them. In later life we look at things in a more practical way, in full conformity with the rest of society, but adolescence is the only period in which we learn anything.

I started this book by giving my reasons for my retirement from teaching at Sands School, and I find myself ending it at much the same point. We can write about anything in the universe, but all we really know is ourselves.

In both my first and last chapters I have mentioned extracts from my diaries of almost 40 years ago, and said how impressed I was by some aspects of my younger self. I am not now merely the same person without the energy, without the sensitivity and without the intellectual alertness. There are gains as well as losses. Although I may feel less intensely and move and think more slowly, I know a great deal more. My role in life has changed, but it is not necessarily less important. Adults need children to remind them of essential moral principles, but the young need the old to remind them of practicalities, to describe circumstances they have not experienced, to bring different points of view to their attention. The old to the young are as the coach to the athlete, the librarian to the inventor, the helmsman to Columbus. We coaches need to get off the field and leave the action to the players, but we are still important.

In *The Philosophy of Childhood* Gareth B. Matthews puts it like this:

Much of philosophy involves giving up adult pretensions to know. The philosopher asks, "What is time, anyway?" when other adults assume, no doubt unthinkingly, that they are well beyond the point of needing to ask that question. They may want to know whether they have enough time to do the week's shopping, or to pick up a newspaper. They may want to know what time it is, but doesn't occur to them to ask, "What is time?" ... Among the annoying questions that children ask are some that are genuinely baffling. In important part, philosophy is an adult attempt to deal with the genuinely baffling questions of childhood.

In important part, the way forward for mankind is for adults to attempt to realise childhood's genuinely baffling ambitions.

What makes me feel optimistic about the present is that today's children are on the whole much more self-confident and self-aware than my generation was at the same age. Whatever the schools may be obliged to do by interfering governments, parents will not be shaken in their new confidence in their offspring, and this gives the children a new confidence in themselves. If they can retain this confidence as they grow older, perhaps when their turn comes – and it will come very soon – they will be able to listen still more readily to those who are younger than they are. From the young they will learn to preserve the altruism with which they were born, not in the form of natural empathy, which probably diminishes with age, but in the form of an appreciation of the need to care for others, and an unforced pleasure in doing so.

Part of the wisdom of age lies in the ability to appreciate the wisdom of the very young. I have made several references to Christianity in the course of this book, usually deploring what I see as misinterpretations of a superb moral code. As I showed in Chapter Eleven, even the religious choose from their religions which parts they wish to believe in. I am not a believer, but to end this book I have chosen a passage from St. Matthew's Gospel. If I had been writing a sermon, this would have been my text. Matthew, chapter eighteen, verses one to three.

And at the same time came the disciples unto Jesus, saying,
Who is the greatest in the kingdom of heaven?

And Jesus called a little child unto him, and set him in the midst of them,
And said, Verily I say unto you, Except ye be converted, and
become as little children, ye shall not enter into the kingdom of heaven.

APPENDIX ONE

A CONTRAST BETWEEN ADULT THINKING
AND CHILDREN'S THINKING

Part of the first sentence of the United Nations Convention on the Rights of the Child, which in full is over 500 words long.

> ... bearing in mind that the need to extend particular care to the child has been stated in the Geneva Declaration of the Rights of the Child in 1924 and in the Declaration on the Rights of the Child adopted by the United Nations on 20 November 1959 and recognized in the Universal Declaration of Human Rights, in the International Covenant on Civil and Political Rights (in particular articles 23 and 24), in the International Covenant on Economic, Social and Cultural Rights (in particular article 10) and in the statutes and relevant instruments of specialized agencies and international organizations concerned with the welfare of children ...

The whole of the first sentence of the Children's Appeal to World Leaders, delivered at the Rio summit on the environment:

We want to inherit a clean earth.

APPENDIX TWO

EXTRACT FROM MY DIARY
WHEN I WAS TWENTY YEARS OLD

21st March, 1953

... Working as a schoolmaster brings me closer to the business about people getting a protective covering or pose as they grow up which hides their true selves and all the beauty of their characters. (That is what I think a pose does.) The pose which occupies the minds of small boys is that of being tough, and in this respect the game of lifesmanship begins early. Almost all of them try to appear "tougher" (in one of the many schoolboy senses) than their neighbours are. Their true emotions come out far more often than an adult's: Freeston was moved to smile and say "How sweet" with real feeling when he saw a picture of a leopard cub in "Jungle Picnic": Hudswell was openly delighted at his little brother's skill in spelling pen, bat and man: almost all the boys are genuinely moved when another boy cries – at least all the smaller boys: Potter and Keller, after a furious quarrel, were quite prepared to become friends again when I told them they were being silly. There are, of course, less pleasant sides to the character underneath: tempers are lost too often, cowardice is made evident in spite of the desire to be tough: scorn and ridiculing I think are part of the pose, already assumed for long enough to have become almost natural. And yet the character as exposed is far nicer than the character of the boy in his mask. Of course habit and automatic reaction are already covering a large part of the boys' reactions, but the semi-conscious mechanism of the pose still breaks down when subjected to the slightest strain.

On thinking over the last part of what I have written it seems to me that in some respects the pose is desirable, as when it promotes courage in stead of cowardice. I think there is some distinction in words which I have failed to make, and I have just said a lot of nonsense. There's some truth hidden in it somewhere, but it will take me a lot of thought to find it out. As so often happens an obvious truth has turned out to be too difficult for me to set down on paper.

I think I was writing sense up as far as the bit about boys being moved by tears. After that I got muddled about what I mean by "pose". I think I mean that all children start with an ideal character, or have an ideal character hidden inside them which is gradually clogged by successive layers of old newspaper. Some of them they put on themselves, others are stuck on them by other people. At the age of eight or nine there are still a lot of gaps in the paper, and nowhere is the paper very thick.

I think that at the public school or possibly at the age of sixteen or fifteen anyway, a lot of the paper is torn off, and is gradually replaced by fresh paper with a different story on it. When a boy leaves school he sets about wrapping himself up in completely blank paper in a desparate attempt to disguise his youth and lack of experience, so making himself into an uninteresting dummy. At the age of twenty-two or three he emerges in a complete papier-mâché armour which is dinted only by the fiercest of blows.

This does not apply to everybody – I am rather nonplussed by the fact that it doesn't seem to apply to any of my real friends – I like to think that that is because I am exceptionally good at getting underneath their protections, but I am probably wrong. Or it may be because I only like people who are not so wrapped up in poses. I think it is a little of both.

APPENDIX THREE

CHILDREN'S APPEAL TO WORLD LEADERS
as presented at the U.N. Conference on Environment and Development
Rio de Janeiro – 1992

WE WANT TO INHERIT A CLEAN EARTH
We would like everybody to understand that the Earth is like a beautiful garden in which no one has the right to destroy anything.
We would like our grandchildren to know: What is a tree, a fish, a dog. Leave us trees to climb in.

ECOLOGY IS NOT JUST TREES, ANIMALS AND RIVERS, IT IS ALSO HUNGER AND THE HOMELESS
We should all help our brothers and sisters who have been abandoned on the streets. Eliminate poverty.
We want you to understand that all excessive consumption affects developing countries most.

WE WANT CHILDREN'S RIGHTS TO BE RESPECTED ALL OVER THE WORLD
No child should be imprisoned or beaten, no child should die of hunger

or from diseases that could easily be prevented. All children have a right to have parents.

WE WANT EVERY GIRL AND BOY IN THE WORLD TO GET AN EDUCATION FOR A BETTER START IN LIFE. WE WANT TO SEE ILLITERACY WIPED OUT

It is our future and we want to have a say in it. We want to be educated in such a way that we get the courage to speak our minds. We want a world without discrimination.

WE WANT VERY STRICT LAWS AGAINST DESTROYING NATURE

Anybody polluting the environment should have to pay large fines. Stop producing materials that harm the ozone layer or it will be broken and the sun's rays will burn us. Stop global warming, reduce CO_2 emissions. Cut the use of fossil fuels, use sun and wind power. Instead of drilling for more oil, use energy less wastefully.

WE WANT YOU TO STOP USING NUCLEAR POWER

End nuclear testing in our oceans and seas, we demand the removal of all nuclear power stations.

WE DON'T WANT OUR CITIES TO BE RUINED BY CARS

We don't want to be sick from exhaust fumes. We want you to make cars that don't pollute. Public transportation should be better, cheaper and more efficient than private cars. Make it easier for us all to use our bicycles.

WE DON'T WANT OUR WORLD TO DROWN IN RUBBISH. NOBODY SHOULD BE ALLOWED TO DUMP THEIR RUBBISH IN OTHER COUNTRIES

Stop littering, make less waste. We don't need all the packaging materials.

WE WOULD LIKE ALL THINGS TO BE RECYCLED

Make it easier for people to recycle their rubbish.
Stop producing disposables.

PLEASE, LEADERS OF THE WORLD, GIVE US CLEAN DRINKING WATER

Without water there is no life. Too many children are drinking clayish water from shallow wells, pipe borne water is still a luxury. Too many children spend hours walking a long way to find water.

WE FEAR THAT WHEN WE GROW UP THERE WILL BE NO FISH IN THE OCEAN

We want you to stop oil spills in the oceans, to stop factories from releasing their sewage and waste into rivers and lakes. The sea cannot absorb poison without being harmed.

ANIMALS HAVE AS MUCH RIGHT TO LIVE ON THIS EARTH AS WE DO

Protect endangered animals, stop buying products made from rare animals. People should be able to do without real fur coats, crocodile leather or jewelry from ivory. Ban animal testing for cosmetics, ban killing animals for sport.

WE WANT MORE DONE TO SAVE WHAT IS LEFT OF THE NATIVE FORESTS

The rainforests are home to many people and animals. We want indigenous peoples to be able to live by their own rules. Don't cut down all the native trees because the birds need homes, just like all the children in the world.

WE ARE AFRAID OF BEING SWEPT OFF THE FACE OF OUR COUNTRY BY THE APPROACHING DESERT

Stop bush-burning and overgrazing that is killing our trees and hurting our grassland vegetation. We want canals to be built alongside the main rivers to prevent flooding. Stop building large dams against people's wishes.

ALL HAVE A RIGHT TO LIVE IN PEACE

The money spent on military armaments should be spent on saving the planet. Instead of making bombs, improve the standard of living in the world.

THE EARTH IS A SINGLE COUNTRY, AND ALL PEOPLE ARE ITS CITIZENS

We have to share this planet, so don't be selfish. We want food to be shared so that everyone has enough. We want clean water and a home for all people. We are worried about pollution, war and children starving, while others don't appreciate the food they get. We are afraid that the world will soon belong only to the rich.

THIS EARTH IS MORE VALUABLE THAN ALL THE MONEY IN THE WORLD. WE WANT ALL COUNTRIES TO WORK TOGETHER TO PROTECT IT.

BIBLIOGRAPHY

Angelou, Maya, *I Know Why the Caged Bird Sings*, Virago, 1984
Barrow, Robin, *Plato, Utilitarianism and Education*, Routledge and Kegan Paul, 1975
Batmanghelidjh, Camila, *Shattered Lives*, Jessica Kingsley Publishers, 2006
Blum, Lawrence, *Friendship, Altruism and Morality*, Routledge and Kegan Paul, 1980
Botwinick, Jack, *Aging and Behaviour*, Springer Publishing Co., 1973
Botwinick, Jack, *Intellectual Abilities*, in *Handbook of the Psychology of Aging*, ed. J. E. Birren and K. W. Schaie, New York, Van Nostrand Reinhold, 1977
Cullingford, Cedric, *Children and Society*, Cassell, 1992
Burningham, John, *A. S. Neill* in the *Heroes and Villains* column of *The Independent*, November 7th 1992
Crowe, Brenda, *Play is a Feeling*, George, Allen and Unwin, 1983
Dawkins, Richard, *The Selfish Gene*, Granada Publishing Ltd., 1978
Douglas, Mary, *How Institutions Think*, Routledge and Kegan Paul, 1987
Dickens, Charles, *Mrs Orange*, Herbert Jenkins, 1948
Dennison, George, *Street Lives*, Penguin Books, 1972
Dunn, Judy, *The Beginnings of Social Understanding*, Basil Blackwell, 1988
Flekkøy, Målfrid Grude, *A Voice for Children*, Jessica Kingsley Publishers, 1991
Forster, E. M., *Howard's End*, Hodder and Stoughton, 1992
Gardner, Howard, *Frames of Mind*, Basic Books, 1983